WORKBOOK

VOLUME
A

FOCUS ON GRAMMAR

A **HIGH-INTERMEDIATE** Course for Reference and Practice

SECOND EDITION

Marjorie Fuchs

Margaret Bonner

Longman

FOCUS ON GRAMMAR: A **HIGH-INTERMEDIATE** COURSE FOR REFERENCE AND PRACTICE
WORKBOOK

Pearson Education, 10 Bank Street, White Plains, NY 10606

Editorial director: Allen Ascher
Executive editor: Louisa Hellegers
Director of design and production: Rhea Banker
Development editor: Randee Falk
Production manager: Alana Zdinak
Managing editor: Linda Moser
Senior production editor: Virginia Bernard
Production editor: Christine Lauricella
Senior manufacturing manager: Patrice Fraccio
Manufacturing manager: David Dickey
Cover design: Rhea Banker
Text design adaptation: Rainbow Graphics
Text composition: Rainbow Graphics
Photo credits: **p.6** PictureQuest; **p.16** AP/Wide World Photos; **p.22** AP/Wide World Photos; **p.52** AP/Wide World Photos

0–201–38307–1

1 2 3 4 5 6 7 8 9 10—BAH—04 03 02 01 00

CONTENTS

ABOUT THE AUTHORS

Marjorie Fuchs has taught ESL at New York City Technical College and LaGuardia Community College of the City University of New York and EFL at the Sprach Studio Lingua Nova in Munich, Germany. She holds a Master's Degree in Applied English Linguistics and a Certificate in TESOL from the University of Wisconsin–Madison. She has authored or co-authored many widely used ESL textbooks, notably *On Your Way: Building Basic Skills in English, Crossroads, Top Twenty ESL Word Games: Beginning Vocabulary Development, Around the World: Pictures for Practice, Families: Ten Card Games for Language Learners, Focus on Grammar: An Intermediate Course for Reference and Practice, Focus on Grammar: A High-Intermediate Course for Reference and Practice,* and the workbooks to the *Longman Dictionary of American English,* the *Longman Photo Dictionary, The Oxford Picture Dictionary,* and the *Vistas* series.

Margaret Bonner has taught ESL at Hunter College and the Borough of Manhattan Community College of the City University of New York, at Taiwan National University in Taipei, and at Virginia Commonwealth University in Richmond. She holds a Master's Degree in Library Science from Columbia University, and she has done work toward a Ph.D. in English Literature at the Graduate Center of the City University of New York. She has contributed to a number of ESL and EFL projects, including *Making Connections, On Your Way,* and the Curriculum Renewal Project in Oman, where she wrote textbooks, workbooks, and teachers manuals for the national school system. She authored *Step into Writing: A Basic Writing Text* and co-authored *Focus on Grammar: An Intermediate Course for Reference and Practice, Focus on Grammar: A High-Intermediate Course for Reference and Practice,* and *The Oxford Picture Dictionary Intermediate Workbook.*

UNIT

1

SIMPLE PRESENT TENSE AND PRESENT PROGRESSIVE

1 SPELLING: SIMPLE PRESENT TENSE AND PRESENT PROGRESSIVE

Write the correct forms of the verbs.

Base Form	Third-Person Singular	Present Participle
1. answer	answers	answering
2. _____	asks	_____
3. _____	_____	beginning
4. bite	_____	_____
5. buy	_____	_____
6. _____	_____	coming
7. dig	_____	_____
8. _____	does	_____
9. _____	_____	employing
10. _____	_____	flying
11. forget	_____	_____
12. _____	has	_____
13. _____	_____	lying
14. manage	_____	_____
15. _____	_____	promising
16. _____	says	_____
17. study	_____	_____
18. _____	_____	traveling
19. use	_____	_____
20. _____	writes	_____

2 SIMPLE PRESENT TENSE AND PRESENT PROGRESSIVE

Complete these conversations with the correct form of the verbs in parentheses.

1. **AMBER:** I _____think_____ I've seen you before. _____ you _____
   a. (think)   b. (take)
   Professor Bertolucci's course this semester?

   NOËL: No, but my twin sister, Dominique, _____ Italian this year.
   c. (study)

   AMBER: That _____ her! I _____ her name now. You two
   d. (be)   e. (remember)
   _____ exactly alike.
   f. (look)

2. **JARED:** _____ you _____ that woman over there?
   a. (know)

   TARO: That's Mangena. She _____ an English class at the Institute.
   b. (take)

   JARED: Mangena. That's an interesting name. What _____ it _____?
   c. (mean)

   TARO: I _____. Let's ask her.
   d. (not know)

3. **ROSA:** How _____ you _____ your name?
   a. (spell)

   ZHUŌ: Here, I'll write it down for you.

   ROSA: You _____ unusual handwriting. It _____ very artistic.
   b. (have)   c. (look)

4. **IVY:** Hi. What _____ you _____? You _____ annoyed.
   a. (do)   b. (seem)

   LEE: I _____ to read this letter from my friend Herb. His handwriting
   c. (try)
   _____ terrible, but he never _____ his letters.
   d. (be)   e. (type)

5. **AMY:** _____ you _____ to hear something interesting? Justin is a
   a. (want)
   graphologist.

   CHRIS: A graphologist? What exactly _____ a graphologist _____?
   b. (do)

   AMY: A graphologist _____ people's handwriting. You can learn a lot
   c. (analyze)
   about people from the way they _____, especially from how they
   d. (write)
   _____ their names.
   e. (sign)

6. **KYLE:** What _____ you _____ these days, Sara?
   a. (do)

   SARA: I _____ an article about graphology.
   b. (write)

   KYLE: Really? I _____ a book about graphology. I _____ it's a
   c. (read)   d. (think)
   fascinating subject.

❸ SIMPLE PRESENT TENSE AND PRESENT PROGRESSIVE

Complete this article with the simple present or present progressive form of the verbs in parentheses.

Right now Pam O'Neil ____is taking____ a test, but she _____ it.
1. (take)   2. (not know)

She _____ about what she _____, not about how her
3. (think)   4. (write)

handwriting _____. The person who will look at the test is a
5. (look)

graphologist—someone who _____ handwriting. Graphologists
6. (study)

_____ that a person's handwriting _____ something
7. (believe)   8. (tell)

about his or her personality and character. These days, many businesses

_____ graphologists to help them decide who to hire.
9. (use)

What exactly _____ company graphologist Perry Vance _____
10. (hope)

to learn from applicants' writing samples? "I always _____ for clues to
11. (look)

possible behavior," he explained. "For example, the slant of the writing usually

_____ a lot. _____ the writing _____ to the left or to
12. (tell)   13. (lean)

the right? A left slant often _____ a shy personality. The position of the
14. (indicate)

sample on the page is also important," Vance continued. "The right-hand margin of

the page _____ the future. Here's a writing sample from an executive who
15. (represent)

right now _____ a new direction for a large company. Notice that this
16. (plan)

person _____ much room in the right-hand margin. This is the writing of
17. (not leave)

someone who never _____ looking at the future."
18. (avoid)

"What about signatures?" I asked. "Yes, signatures _____ us a lot about
19. (show)

someone," said Vance. "Look at this one by a chief executive officer of a large firm.

You _____ about him in the news these days because the government
20. (read)

_____ his company. Those very large strokes are typical of a person who
21. (investigate)

_____ about himself first and _____ advantage of other people.
22. (think)   23. (take)

Vance always _____, however, that his analysis _____ an
24. (warn)   25. (not guarantee)

applicant's future job performance. There's no substitute for careful review of a

complete application.

❹ EDITING

Read this e-mail. Find and correct ten mistakes in the use of the simple present tense and the present progressive. The first mistake is already corrected.

Justin—I hope you ~~don't~~ *aren't* feeling angry at me about my last e-mail. Remember that I

wrote, "I not want to hear from you again! '-)" That little symbol at the end means,

"I'm winking, and I only joke." We using a lot of these symbols in e-mail. We are

calling them emoticons because they show how we are feeling at the moment.

Here are some more:

:-)	I smile.
:-D	I'm laughing.
:-(	I'm frowning.
8-]	Wow! I really surprised!
(:: ( ) ::)	This is meaning, "I want to help." It looks like a Band-Aid.
:-C	I'm not believing that!

Please write back soon and tell me that your not angry. ((((Justin)))) Those are hugs!

Delia

SIMPLE PAST TENSE AND PAST PROGRESSIVE

① SPELLING: REGULAR AND IRREGULAR SIMPLE PAST TENSE FORMS

Write the correct forms of the verbs.

Base Form	Past Tense
1. _____*agree*_____	agreed
2. _____	applied
3. be	_____ OR _____
4. become	_____
5. develop	_____
6. _____	ate
7. _____	felt
8. get	_____
9. grow	_____
10. live	_____
11. _____	met
12. _____	paid
13. permit	_____
14. plan	_____
15. say	_____
16. _____	sent
17. sleep	_____
18. understand	_____

② SIMPLE PAST TENSE, PAST PROGRESSIVE, AND *WAS/WERE GOING TO*

Complete the magazine article with the correct forms of the verbs in parentheses. Choose the simple past tense, the past progressive, or **was/were going to**.

First Meetings

by Rebecca Hubbard

*W*hat ___were___ you ___doing___
                    1. (do)
when you first _____ that special person
                2. (meet)
in your life? A few months ago, we _____
                                     3. (ask)
couples to tell us about themselves. _____
                                      4. (Be)
it love at first sight or _____ you

_____ each other? _____
5. (hate)
you _____ someone else before you
      6. (marry)
_____ your One True Love? Read some of the great stories from our readers.
7. (find)

*D*ana and I sure _____ in love at first sight! We _____ in the
                  8. (not fall)   **9. (work)**
same office when we _____. At the time the company _____
                    10. (meet)   **11. (hire)**
me, she _____ to get a promotion. It _____ my first job. I
        12. (try)   **13. (be)**
_____ scared, so I _____ to know everything. Of course,
14. (feel)   **15. (pretend)**
Dana _____ I _____ to get the promotion instead of her.
     16. (think)   **17. (want)**

One day I _____ on a problem when she _____ into my office. I
    18. (work)   **19. (come)**

_____ her for help, but I was stuck, so finally I did. And guess what? She
20. (not ask)

_____ it! So then we _____ competing with each other and
21. (solve)   **22. (stop)**

_____ in love instead.
23. (fall)

*V*an and I _____ the same high school social studies class when
           24. (take)

we _____. We _____ friends right away. At the time, I
  25. (meet)   **26. (become)**

_____ someone else, and Van _____ interested in a romantic
27. (date)   **28. (not seem)**

relationship. One day the teacher _____ me while I _____ to Van.
        29. (hear)   **30. (whisper)**

Because of that, we both _____ stay after school. I _____ about
        31. (have to)   **32. (complain)**

such a severe punishment, but I _____ my mind because staying late with a
        33. (change)

friend _____ so bad. That afternoon, we _____ talking. As soon
  34. (not be)   **35. (not stop)**

as I _____ with my old boyfriend, I _____ Van out.
36. (break up)   **37. (ask)**

*A*leesha _____ into the apartment next door when I _____ her
  38. (move)   **39. (see)**

for the first time. I _____ on the front steps while she _____ a
      40. (sit)   **41. (park)**

U-Haul in front of the apartment building. As soon as she _____ out of the
        42. (jump)

truck, I _____, "I'm going to marry that woman." I _____ her out
43. (think)   **44. (ask)**

right away, but a guy _____ her move. He _____ like her
      45. (help)   **46. (look)**

boyfriend. But I _____ my plan to marry her. One day, I _____
47. (not give up)   **48. (run into)**

Aleesha and her "boyfriend" in the hall. She _____ me to her *brother!* I
        49. (introduce)

_____ her to dinner the next weekend.
50. (invite)

❸ EDITING

Read this entry from Aleesha's journal. Find and correct ten mistakes in the use of the simple past tense, the past progressive, and **was/were going to**. *The first mistake is already corrected.*

> *December 16*
>
>   *decided*
>   *I'm really glad that I ~~was deciding~~ to rent this apartment. I won't*
>
> *move here because the rent is a little high, but I'm happy I did. All the*
>
> *others were seeming so small, and the neighborhoods just weren't as*
>
> *beautiful as this one. And moving wasn't as bad as I feared. I was*
>
> *planning to take more days off work, but then Hakim offers to help.*
>
> *What a great brother! We were moving everything into the apartment in*
>
> *two days. The man next door seemed really nice. On the second day, he*
>
> *even help Hakim with some of the heavy furniture. His name is Jared. I*
>
> *don't even unpack the kitchen stuff last weekend because I was so tired.*
>
> *Last night I walking Mitzi for only two blocks. Jared was standing*
>
> *downstairs and looked at his mail when I came back. I was going to*
>
> *asked him over for dinner this weekend (in order to thank him), but*
>
> *everything is still in boxes. Maybe in a couple of weeks . . .*

PRESENT PERFECT, PRESENT PERFECT PROGRESSIVE, AND SIMPLE PAST TENSE

1 SPELLING: SIMPLE PAST TENSE AND PRESENT PERFECT

Write the correct forms of the verbs.

Base Form	Past Tense	Past Participle
1. become	*became*	*become*
2. bring		
3. choose		
4. delay		
5. feel		
6. find		
7. finish		
8. get		
9. graduate		
10. hide		
11. move		
12. notice		
13. own		
14. read		
15. reply		
16. rip		
17. show		
18. speak		
19. throw		
20. wonder		

❷ CONTRAST: PRESENT PERFECT, PRESENT PERFECT PROGRESSIVE, AND SIMPLE PAST TENSE

Look at the reporter's notes about the bride's and the groom's families.
Then write sentences about them, using the words in parentheses.
Choose the present perfect, present perfect progressive, or simple past
tense form of the verbs. Add any necessary words to the time expressions.

THE SKOAP–POHLIG WEDDING BACKGROUND INFORMATION	
Bride	*Groom*
Nakisha Skoap	Simon Pohlig
born in Broadfield	moved to Broadfield in 1992
lived here all her life	bought Sharney's Restaurant in 1994
B.A., Claremont College, 1994	basketball coach for Boys and Girls Club
1991–Began working for	1997-1999
Broadfield Examiner	author, <u>Simon Says</u> and <u>Duck Soup,</u>
1997–became crime news reporter	kids' cookbooks
and started Master's Degree	in Jan., started developing local
program in Political Science	TV show
started research on articles on crime	Mother–Tina Pohlig, president of
in schools in Jan.	TLC Meals, Inc., for two
Father–James Skoap, joined the	years, but plans to retire soon
Broadfield Police Department	
in 1979, retired in 1999	

1. (Nakisha Skoap / live in Broadfield / all her life)

　　Nakisha Skoap has lived in Broadfield all her life.

2. (she / graduate / from college / 1994)

_____

3. (report / crime news / 1997)

_____

4. (recently, / research / articles about crime in schools)

_____

5. (work / on her Master's Degree / 1997)

_____

6. (her father / work / for the Broadfield Police Department / twenty years)

_____

7. (Simon Pohlig / move / to Broadfield / 1992)

_____

8. (own / Sharney's Restaurant / 1994)

_____

9. (coach / basketball / for the Boys and Girls Club / two years)

_____

10. (write / two cookbooks for children)

_____

11. (plan / local television show / several months)

_____

12. (the groom's mother / serve as / president of TLC Meals, Inc., / two years)

_____

❸ PRESENT PERFECT, PRESENT PERFECT PROGRESSIVE, AND SIMPLE PAST TENSE

Look at Nakisha's job application. Then complete the personnel officer's notes, using the correct form of the verbs in parentheses. Choose between the affirmative and negative form.

CODEX MAGAZINES JOB APPLICATION

1. **Position applied for** _____ Editor _____ **Today's Date:** Nov. 12, 1999

2. **Full legal name** __ Skoap-Pohlig __ Nakisha __ Ann __
                        Last   First   Middle

3. **Current address** _____ 22 East 10th Street _____

   __ Broadfield, __ Ohio __ 43216 __ **How long at this address?** _5 months_
        City   State   Zip Code

4. **Previous address** _____ 17 Willow Terrace _____

   __ Broadfield, __ Ohio __ 43216 __ **How long at this address?** _1968–June 1, 1999_
        City   State   Zip Code

5. **Education.** Circle the number of years of post high school education. 1 2 3 4 5 6 ⑦ 8

6.

Name of Institution	Degree	Major	Dates Attended
1. Claremont College	B.A.	Journalism	1990–1994
2. Ohio State University	——	Urban Studies	1996
3. Ohio State University		Political Science	1997–present

   If you expect to complete an educational program soon, indicate the date and type of program.

   __ I expect to receive my M.S. in Political Science in January. __

7. **Current job.** May we contact your present supervisor? _____ yes _X_ no

   Job Title _Reporter_   **Employer** _Broadfield Examiner_

   Type of Business _newspaper_   **Address** _1400 River Street, Broadfield, OH 43216_

   Dates (month/year) _9/91_   **to (month/year)** _present_

8. In your own handwriting, describe your duties and what you find most satisfying in this job.

   __ I am currently a crime reporter for a daily newspaper. I write local crime news. I especially enjoy __

   __ working with my supervisor. __

1. I <u>'ve interviewed</u> Nakisha Skoap-Pohlig for the editorial position.
  (interview)

2. She _____ for a job on November 12.
  (apply)

3. She _____ at the *Broadfield Examiner* for a long time.
  (work)

4. She _____ that job while she _____ a college student.
  (find)   (be)

5. She _____ two schools of higher education.
  (attend)

6. She _____ classes at Claremont College in 1990 and _____ her
  (begin)   (receive)

  B.A. there.

7. Then she _____ to Ohio State University.
  (go on)

8. She _____ Ohio State University for three years.
  (attend)

9. At Ohio State, she _____ Urban Studies.
  (take)

10. She _____ a degree in Urban Studies, though.
  (get)

11. After a year, she _____ to study Political Science instead.
  (decide)

12. She _____ her Master's Degree yet.
  (receive)

13. She _____ at Willow Terrace most of her life.
  (live)

14. For the past five months, she _____ on East 10th Street.
  (live)

15. The company graphologist _____ at her application yesterday.
  (look)

16. He says that in question 8 of the application, Ms. Skoap-Pohlig _____ a space
  (leave)

  between some words when she _____ her supervisor.
  (mention)

17. She probably _____ her supervisor yet about looking for a new job.
  (tell)

18. In her answer to question 8, she _____ her writing to either the left or the
  (slant)

  right.

19. The graphologist _____ me yesterday that this indicates clear and
  (tell)

  independent thinking.

20. The graphologist _____ that we contact this applicant for another interview.
  (suggest)

4 EDITING

*Read this letter to an advice column. Find and correct fourteen mistakes
in the use of the present perfect, present perfect progressive, and simple
past tense. The first mistake is already corrected.*

Dear John,

    My son and his girlfriend ~~have made~~ *have been making* wedding plans for the past few months.
At first I was delighted, but last week I have heard something that changed my
feelings. It seems that our future daughter-in-law has been deciding to keep her
own last name after the wedding. Her reasons: First, she doesn't want to "lose her
identity." Her parents have named her 21 years ago, and she was Donna Esposito
since then. She sees no reason to change now. Second, she is a member of the
Rockland Symphony Orchestra and she performed with them for eight years.
As a result, she already became known professionally by her maiden name.

    John, when I've gotten married, I didn't think of keeping my maiden name.
I have felt so proud when I became "Mrs. Smith." We named our son after my
father, but our surname showed that we three were a family.

    I've been reading two articles about this trend, and I can now understand her
decision to use her maiden name professionally. But I still can't understand why
she wants to use it socially.

    My husband and I tried to hide our hurt feelings, but it's been getting harder.
I want to tell her and my son what I think, but my husband says it's none of our
business.

    My son didn't say anything, so we don't know how he feels. Have we been
making the right choice by keeping quiet?

HASN'T BEEN SAYING ONE WORD YET

PAST PERFECT AND
PAST PERFECT PROGRESSIVE

4

1 SPELLING: REGULAR AND IRREGULAR PAST PARTICIPLES

Write the correct forms of the verbs.

Base Form	Past Participle
1. do	*done*
2. _fight_	fought
3. entertain	_____
4. cut	_____
5. tell	_____
6. _____	withdrawn
7. practice	_____
8. worry	_____
9. _____	sought
10. sweep	_____
11. quit	_____
12. lead	_____
13. _____	written
14. steal	_____
15. plan	_____
16. _____	broken
17. swim	_____
18. bet	_____
19. _____	sunk
20. forgive	_____

2 PAST PERFECT: AFFIRMATIVE AND NEGATIVE STATEMENTS

Complete the information about late-night TV talk-show host David Letterman. Use the past perfect form of the verbs in parentheses and choose between affirmative and negative.

Better Late Than Never

by Manuel Salazar

David Letterman

Late-night TV host David Letterman, often described as an "observational comic," is famous for his comments on everyday life. Even as a young child, Letterman ____had shown____ natural
1. (show)
comic abilities, entertaining family and friends. Family has always been important to Letterman. His father died when Letterman was twenty-seven. They _____ a close relationship, and Letterman
2. (enjoy)
felt the loss deeply.

After getting his degree in radio and TV broadcasting, Letterman worked as a TV announcer and radio talk-show host. Once he substituted for a television weatherman but left after only two weeks because he _____ bored and _____ to
3. (become)   **4. (start)**
draw objects in the clouds. He _____ even _____ disasters in cities
5. (invent)
that didn't exist. Letterman was fired. The network _____ his creative reporting.
6. (appreciate)
In 1975, Letterman left for Los Angeles, along with six TV comedy scripts he

_____. No one was interested in them. In 1977, he was hired as a writer and
7. (write)
performer on a variety show. That same year, he got divorced from his college sweetheart.

The couple _____ married for nine years.
8. (be)
Letterman was soon discovered by one of Johnny Carson's talent scouts, who

_____ him perform on the short-lived TV comedy "Mary." Carson, the "king"
9. (see)
of late-night TV, first invited Letterman to appear on his program, "The Tonight Show,"

in November 1978. Although Letterman _____ late-night TV before, he

10. (do)

quickly became Carson's most frequent guest host.

Two years later, Letterman got his own show, which went on the air at 10:00 A.M.

Although the show _____ favorable reviews, it was canceled after only eighteen

11. (get)

weeks. The ratings _____ high, perhaps because of the morning time slot.

12. (be)

In 1982, Letterman was given his own "Late Night with David Letterman" directly

following Carson's show. Later, when Carson announced his plans to retire, Letterman and

comedian Jay Leno competed to take over "The Tonight Show." By the time Carson

actually left, the struggle _____ to the point where it was dominating both

13. (grow)

entertainment and business news. Network TV _____ anything like it before.

14. (see)

When "The Tonight Show" was finally offered to Leno, Letterman changed networks,

to CBS. He _____ it clear to NBC that he would accept nothing less than the

15. (make)

job as host of "The Tonight Show." "The Late Show" plays opposite Leno's "The Tonight

Show" and so far has gotten higher ratings—giving the last laugh to Letterman, after all.

❸ PAST PERFECT: *YES/NO* QUESTIONS AND SHORT ANSWERS

Look at David Letterman's schedule. Ask and answer questions about it.

A.M.

○   *get up*
      go for jog
      drive to New York City
 10:30—arrive at the studio

○   *work with staff and crew*
P.M.

○   *tape evening show*
      meet with producers
      drive back to Connecticut
      dinner

○   *watch TV*   *10:30—go to bed*

Source: Based on information from Caroline Latham, "Does Anyone Know the Real David Letterman?" *Cosmopolitan*, January 1987.

(continued on next page)

1. It was 11:00 A.M.

    A: _____Had he gotten up_____ yet?

    B: _____Yes, he had._____

2. Letterman was going for his morning jog.

    A: _____ to New York yet?

    B: _____

3. It was 9:00 A.M.

    A: _____ at the studio by then?

    B: _____

4. It was noon.

    A: _____ for a jog yet?

    B: _____

5. It was late afternoon.

    A: _____ with his staff and crew by then?

    B: _____

6. At 1:00 Letterman was still working with his staff.

    A: _____ with the producers yet?

    B: _____

7. At 6:00 Letterman met with the producers.

    A: _____ the evening show yet?

    B: _____

8. Letterman was on his way home to Connecticut.

    A: _____ dinner yet?

    B: _____

9. "Late Night" was on TV at 12:30 A.M.

    A: _____ to bed yet?

    B: _____

4 SIMPLE PAST TENSE AND PAST PERFECT IN TIME CLAUSES

Jay Leno is another late-night TV talk-show host. This timeline shows some important events in his life.

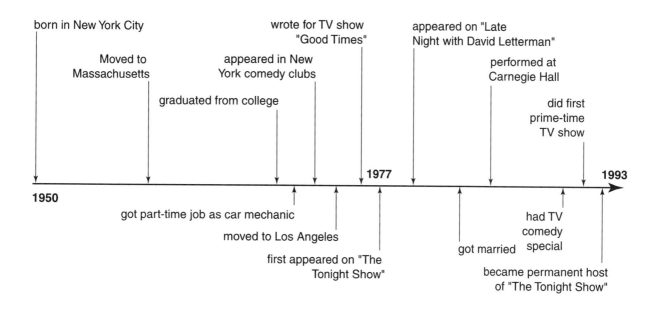

Use the timeline to determine the correct order of the events below. Then combine the phrases, using the past perfect to express the event that occurred first. Use commas when necessary.

1. moved to Massachusetts / graduated from college

By the time ___he graduated from college, he had moved to Massachusetts.___

2. appeared in New York City comedy clubs / got a part-time job as a car mechanic

Before _____

3. moved to Los Angeles / wrote for TV

_____ after _____

4. appeared on "The Tonight Show" / wrote for the TV show "Good Times"

By the time _____

5. appeared on "The Tonight Show" / appeared on "Late Night with David Letterman"

_____ before _____

6. got married / appeared on "Late Night with David Letterman"

When _____ already _____

(continued on next page)

7. did his first prime-time TV show / performed at Carnegie Hall

By the time _____

8. had a TV comedy special / did his first prime-time TV show

_____ by the time _____

9. became the permanent host of "The Tonight Show" / appeared on "The Tonight Show"

many times

_____ when _____

**5 PAST PERFECT PROGRESSIVE:
AFFIRMATIVE AND NEGATIVE STATEMENTS**

*Read the situations. Use the past perfect progressive form of the correct
verbs from the box to draw conclusions. Choose between affirmative
and negative forms.*

cry	do	drink	eat	interview	laugh
listen	pay	rain	tell	wash	~~watch~~

1. When I got home, Mara wasn't in the living room, but the TV was on.

_____ She had been watching _____ TV.

2. The lights were off, and none of her schoolbooks were around.

She _____ homework.

3. "The Tonight Show" was on. The audience was laughing.

Jay Leno _____ jokes.

4. The window was open, and the floor was a little wet.

It _____

5. There was half a sandwich on the coffee table.

Mara _____ the sandwich.

6. There was an unopened bottle of soda next to the sandwich.

She _____ the soda.

7. Mara entered the room. There were tears on her face.

At first I thought she _____

8. I was wrong. Mara wasn't upset.

She _____ hard at Leno's jokes.

9. There was a stack of clean plates in the kitchen sink.

She _____ dishes.

10. Mara could hear the TV from the kitchen.

She _____ to Leno's jokes from the kitchen.

11. The show was almost over. Leno was thanking one of his guests.

He _____ comedian Margaret Cho.

12. I was surprised that the show was almost over.

I _____ attention to the time.

6 PAST PERFECT PROGRESSIVE: QUESTIONS AND SHORT ANSWERS

Complete these conversations with the past perfect progressive form of the verbs in parentheses and with short answers.

1. A: Did you enjoy the show?

   B: Yes. It was great to finally get to see Leno live.

   A: _____Had_____ you _____been waiting_____ a long time
   to get tickets?
   (wait)

   B: _____. I'm from out of town, so it was difficult to get

   tickets for the nights I could come.

2. A: When you came out of the theater, you had tears in your eyes.

   _____ you _____?
   (cry)

   B: _____. Those were tears of laughter!

3. A: Did you enjoy Leno's guests?

   B: Yes. That Margaret Cho is really pretty funny!

   A: _____ you _____ to find her
   so funny?
   (expect)

   B: _____. I had never even heard of her before.

(continued on next page)

4. A: You two looked very serious when you walked out the door.

　　　_____ you _____?
　　　　　　　　　　　　　　　　　　　　　　　　　　　(argue)

　B: _____. My husband thought that Leno shouldn't joke

　　　about certain topics. I disagreed. We always have the same argument.

5. A: Cho said she had just returned to Los Angeles.

　B: _____ she _____?
　　　　　　　　　　　　　　　　　　　　　　　　　　(travel)

　A: _____. She had been on tour in Canada. She likes to

　　　perform at college campuses.

6. A: When we got out of the theater, the ground was all wet.

　B: _____ it _____ ?
　　　　　　　　　　　　　　　　　　　　　　　　　　(rain)

　A: _____. I guess the theater owners had decided to wash the

　　　streets while we were inside.

7 PAST PERFECT AND PAST PERFECT PROGRESSIVE

*Complete this article with the past perfect or past perfect progressive
form of the verbs in parentheses. Use the past perfect progressive when
possible.*

Queen of Comedy

by Yoon Song

Margaret Cho was born in San Francisco on December 5,

1968. Her parents _____*had left*_____ Korea and
　　　　　　　　　　1. (leave)

_____ to the United States four
　　2. (immigrate)

years before. Cho grew up in San Francisco, where she

attended the High School of Performing Arts and a theater

program at San Francisco State University. By the time she

won her first comedy contest, she _____ regularly at a
                                        3. (perform)
comedy club located above her parents' bookstore. Cho _____
                                                            4. (work)
for her parents and _____ upstairs to perform during her
                            5. (go)
breaks.

In 1992, Cho moved to Los Angeles. There she won the American Comedy Award

for Top Female Comedian. At the time, she _____ students
                                                6. (entertain)
for two years with her stand-up comedy, which she performed on college campuses.

Cho was becoming very popular.

By the time she got her own TV comedy series, "All-American Girl," she

_____ already _____ on Arsenio
                                            7. (appear)
Hall's late-night talk show. Cho _____ a long and
                                        8. (count on)
successful show, but her series was canceled after only six months. As the first series

featuring an Asian family, it _____ a lot of controversy.
                                    9. (create)
Some people felt that the show _____ Asians accurately.
                                    10. (not represent)
Cho was very disappointed, but she _____ a lot from the
                                        11. (learn)
experience. She has continued performing at clubs and theaters and on college

campuses and has appeared on all the major late-night talk shows. When asked about

her goals, Cho says, "There's a great lack of different faces out there. I think part of

my journey has to be illustrating my experience. . . . I've gotten to a great place in

my life. I just want to do it for a long time."

UNIT

FUTURE AND FUTURE PROGRESSIVE

① CONTRAST OF FUTURE FORMS

Read the conversations between two neighbors. Circle the most appropriate future forms.

1. **A:** Hi, Jan. What are you doing?

   B: Packing. We'll move / (We're moving) tomorrow.

2. **A:** Do you need any help?

   B: I could use a hand.

   A: Fine. I'll come / I'm going to come right away.

3. **A:** Do you take / Are you taking the refrigerator?

   B: No. Our new house already has one.

4. **A:** I can't reach that vase.

   B: No problem. I'm handing / I'll hand it to you.

5. **A:** Watch out! It'll fall / It's going to fall!

   B: Don't worry. I've got it.

6. **A:** You're moving / You'll move out of state, aren't you?

   B: Yes. To Boston.

7. **A:** Are you driving / Do you drive there?

   B: No. We'll fly / We're flying.

8. **A:** How are you getting / do you get to the airport?

   B: We're going to take / We take a taxi.

9. **A:** Oh, don't take a taxi. I'm driving / I'll drive you.

   B: Thank you! I hope we're having / we're going to have neighbors as

   nice as you in our new neighborhood!

❷ FUTURE PROGRESSIVE: AFFIRMATIVE AND NEGATIVE STATEMENTS

Complete this article with the future progressive form of the verbs in parentheses. Choose affirmative or negative.

An Old Approach to a New Problem

Next year, Azize and Kiral Yazgan _____will be moving_____ from their
                                                1. (move)
rented two-bedroom city apartment to a place called Glenn Commons. There they

_____ in one of a row of houses facing other houses, all
          2. (live)
without fences or hedges. They _____ in an area in back of
                                                3. (park)
the houses. And even though there is a nice kitchen with a large window, the Yazgans

_____ dinners there. Azize, Kiral, and their two children
          4. (prepare)
_____ most evening meals along with twenty other
          5. (eat)
families in a common house. And they _____ there.
                                                6. (drive)
They _____ along paths and greenery.
          7. (walk)
   This doesn't sound like the suburbs. What's going on? The Yazgans, along with a

growing number of other people, _____ to one of the many
                                                8. (move)
planned communities that are now being built around the world. Called "co-housing,"

these communities have cooperative living arrangements that avoid some of the

isolation and loneliness of suburban life.

   While the Yazgans get to know their neighbors, they _____

also _____ money. For starters, they _____
          9. (save)   10. (buy)
a lawn mower or a washer-dryer since the community shares large equipment. And they

_____ food, utility, or child care bills as individuals either.
          11. (pay)

(continued on next page)

Child care? Yes. The Yazgans _____ anymore about what to

<u>12. (worry)</u>

do when one of their children has a cold and each parent is due at a business meeting in

an hour. The center _____ for that.

<u>13. (provide)</u>

The Yazgans will, however, have some added responsibilities. For one thing, they will

have to be much more involved in their community. Even before they move in, they

_____ monthly meetings to decide how the community is

<u>14. (attend)</u>

run. And several times a month they _____ to prepare the

<u>15. (help)</u>

dinners and _____ the child care for others. It's clearly not a

<u>16. (provide)</u>

lifestyle that will appeal to everyone.

Who started this new idea? Actually, the idea itself is quite old, going back to

nineteenth-century European villages. Co-housing has been used in Denmark since

1972. Even though only a few co-housing communities have been completed in Canada,

Europe, the United States, and New Zealand, we _____ more

<u>17. (see)</u>

and more of them in the near future as people try to improve the quality of their lives by

returning to some of the values of the past.

❸ FUTURE PROGRESSIVE: QUESTIONS AND SHORT ANSWERS

*Use the future progressive or short answers to complete these
conversations that take place at a co-housing meeting. Use negative
forms when necessary.*

1. (when / we / plant the garden?)

 A: <u>When will we be planting the garden?</u>

 B: Jack's bought the seed, so we should be ready to start this week.

2. Speaking of gardening, Martha, (you / use the lawn mower tomorrow?)

 A: _____

 B: _____. You can have it if you'd like.

3. You know, with more families moving in, the laundry facilities aren't adequate

anymore. (when / we / get new washers?)

A: _____

B: The housing committee is getting information on brands and prices. They'll be

ready to report on them at the next meeting.

4. Jack, (you / go to the post office / tomorrow?)

A: _____

B: _____. Can I mail something for you?

5. Eun, you and Bon-Hua are in charge of dinner Friday night. (what / you / make?)

A: _____

B: How does vegetable soup, roast chicken, corn bread, salad, and chocolate chip

cookies sound?

6. (who / watch the kids tomorrow?)

A: _____

Al was supposed to do it, but he's still sick.

B: That's no problem. I can take care of them.

7. (the entertainment committee / plan anything else in the near future?)

A: _____

I really enjoyed that slide show last month.

B: _____. We're thinking of organizing a square dance.

8. As you know, this is my husband's and my first meeting. (we / meet every month?)

A: _____

B: _____. Meetings take place the fifteenth of every month.

9. I was just looking at my calendar. The fifteenth of next month is a Sunday. (we / meet

then?)

A: _____

B: _____. When the fifteenth falls on a weekend, we switch

the meeting to the following Monday.

4 FUTURE PROGRESSIVE OR SIMPLE PRESENT TENSE

Look at Azize and Kiral Yazgan's schedules for tomorrow. Complete the statements.

Azize

8:00 go to the post office

9:00 fax reports

10:00 have phone conference with John Smith

11:00 work on the Jansen report

12:00 lunch with Sara Neumann

1:00 bill clients

4:00 take Saril to the dentist

5:00 shop for food

7:00 pay bills

Kiral

8:00 take the car in for inspection

9:00 meet with the boss

10:00 attend the time-management seminar

11:00

12:00 lunch with Jack Allen

1:00 draft the A & W proposal

4:00 pick up the car

5:00 take Dursan to the barber

7:00 cut the grass

1. While Azize _____ goes to _____ the post office, Kiral ___ will be taking the car in for inspection ___.

2. Kiral _____ his boss while Azize

_____ .

3. While Kiral _____ a time-management seminar, Azize

_____ .

4. While Azize _____ lunch with Sara Neumann, Kiral

_____ .

5. Azize _____ while Kiral _____

_____ the A & W proposal.

6. While Kiral _____ the car, Azize

_____ .

7. Azize _____ food while Kiral

_____ .

8. While Azize _____ the bills, Kiral

_____ .

5 EDITING

Read Kiral's note to Azize. Find and correct seven mistakes in the use of the future and the future progressive. The first mistake is already corrected.

> *8:00 p.m.*
>
> Azize—
>   'm going
> I ~~go~~ to Jack's with the kids in a few minutes. We'll be play cards
>
> until 10:30 or so. While we'll play cards, Jack's daughter will be
>
> watching the kids.
>
> It will rain, so I closed all the windows.
>
> Don't forget to watch "ER"! It'll start at 10:00.
>
> I call you after the card game because by the time we get home
>
> you're sleeping.
>
> Enjoy your evening!
>
> Love,
>
> K

FUTURE PERFECT AND FUTURE PERFECT PROGRESSIVE

1 AFFIRMATIVE AND NEGATIVE STATEMENTS

Complete the article with the future perfect or the future perfect progressive form of the verbs in parentheses.

As of December this year, Pam and Jessica Weiner

_____will have been working_____ as personal time-management
        1. (work)

consultants for five years. Tired of disorganization at home, Pam and

Jessica developed a system that worked so well that they started

teaching it to others. By this anniversary celebration, hundreds of

people _____ the Weiners' seminars, and
        2. (complete)

these efficient sisters _____ them manage
        3. (help)

the confusion in their personal lives.

    "What a difference their seminars made!" exclaimed Corinne

Smith, who completed the course a few years ago. "This December,

I _____ their system for two years. I
        4. (use)

used to do my holiday shopping on December 23. This year, I

_____ all my gifts by November 1,
        5. (buy)

and I _____ them too."
        6. (wrap)

    Why do we need a system? "Our lives are so complicated

that we can't remember it all," explained Pam Weiner. "A good

example is a new family in our seminar. They have two children,

they both work, but they have no system. By Monday, they

_____ the week's menu, and they
        7. (not plan)

_____ on a driving schedule for the week's activities.

8. (not decide)

That means that by Friday, they _____ probably

_____ for days about these things."

9. (argue)

The Metcalfs, one of many satisfied families, feel that their life has

improved a lot since they finished the seminars. "At the end of this week,

we _____ our energy arguing about who does

10. (not waste)

what in the house," Aida Metcalf told us. "And we can plan for fun activities. We

know that we _____ all the housework by Saturday,

11. (complete)

and we can make plans to go out. When we go back to work on Monday, we

_____ a good time for two days, and we'll feel

12. (have)

refreshed."

The system also works for long-range planning. "Before the seminars, our

summers were a nightmare," Aida says. "We never did the things we wanted to

do. But by the end of August this year, we _____ in

13. (participate)

our community yard sale and _____ the house. And I

14. (redecorate)

can be sure that we _____ all the preparations for our

15. (make)

September family get-together."

Children enjoy using the system, too. "I made a calendar for Corrie, our

twelve-year-old," reported Arnie Metcalf. "By the time she gets on the school

bus tomorrow morning, she _____ several chores. She

16. (do)

_____ her room, for example, and probably, she

17. (straighten)

_____ her own lunch as well."

18. (pack)

The Weiners are scheduled to appear on tomorrow's "Around Town," and this

also represents a kind of anniversary for them. "Our television appearances

started with this show," Pam Weiner told us. "As of tomorrow, we

_____ our system to televison audiences for a year."

19. (explain)

❷ QUESTIONS AND RESPONSES

Complete the conversations with short answers or the future perfect or
future perfect progressive form of the verbs in parentheses.

1. A: I'm going shopping. 'Bye.

   B: I have to leave at two o'clock for a dentist appointment.

   _____Will_____ you _____have brought_____ the car back by then?
                                              (bring)
   A: _____. I don't have much to buy.

2. A: Corrie, your group is singing at the fund raiser next weekend, right? By three

   o'clock, how long _____ you _____?
                                                                    (sing)
   B: About half an hour. Why?

   A: There's a rock band from the high school that wants to start at three.

3. A: This is Aida. I'm in charge of the handicrafts booth this year. How many

   of those nice dish towels _____ you _____ by
                                                                          (sew)
   Sunday? Do you know?

   B: Oh, at least twenty.

4. A: Oh, no. I forgot about carpooling today.

   B: Suppose you leave right now. How long _____ the kids

   _____ by the time you get there?
        (wait)
   A: Only about fifteen minutes. I guess that's not a big deal.

5. A: Arnie, _____ the paint _____ downstairs
                                                                (dry)
   by the fifteenth?

   B: _____. We'd better give it until the sixteenth. Why?

   A: I want to hang the curtains.

6. A: _____ the cleaners _____ them by then?
                                                        (deliver)
   B: _____. They promised me I'd have them on the twelfth.

7. A: Do you realize that September first is an anniversary? That's the date we moved into

   this house.

   B: How many years _____ we _____ here?
                                                              (live)
   A: Ten. Amazing, isn't it?

❸ QUESTIONS AND AFFIRMATIVE STATEMENTS

Look at the Metcalfs' calendar for August. Write questions and answers about their activities. Choose between the future perfect and the future perfect progressive.

August

Sunday	Monday	Tuesday	Wednesday	Thursday	Friday	Saturday
1 Aida walk 1/2 mi every day	**2** Arnie paint first bedroom	**3** Arnie paint second bedroom	**4** Arnie paint bathroom	**5** Aida start driving in carpool for day camp	**6**	**7**
8 Aida water garden daily	**9** Start picking vegetables daily	**10**	**11** Arnie paint downstairs	**12** - - - - - - - ▶	**13**	**14**
15 Arnie finish painting indoors	**16** Arnie 4:00 P.M. dentist appointment	**17** Corrie pick blueberries for pies (need 3 quarts)	**18**	**19** Aida start baking pies for bake sale (agreed to bring 6 pies)	**20**	**21** Bake sale for fund raiser at Community Center
22 Aida start unpacking fall clothing - - - - ▶	**23**	**24**	**25** Iron and put away fall clothing	**26** Last day of carpool	**27**	**28**
29 Aida and Arnie pack for trip to Mom and Dad's - - - ▶	**30**	**31** Travel to Mom and Dad's - - - - - ▶				

---

1. (how many miles / Aida / walk / by August 31?)

A: How many miles will Aida have walked by August 31?

B: She'll have walked 15 1/2 miles.

(continued on next page)

2. (how long / Aida / walk / by August 31?)

      A: _____

      B: _____

3. (how many rooms / Arnie / paint / by August 5?)

      A: _____

      B: _____

4. (how long / Arnie / paint downstairs / by August 15?)

      A: _____

      B: _____

5. (on August 16, / Arnie / leave / for his dentist appointment / by four o'clock?)

      A: _____

      B: _____

6. (Aida / unpack / all the fall clothing / by August 23?)

      A: _____

      B: _____

7. (how long / Aida / drive in the carpool / by August 19?)

      A: _____

      B: _____

8. (how many quarts of blueberries / Corrie / pick / by August 19?)

      A: _____

      B: _____

9. (how many pies / Aida / bake / by August 21?)

      A: _____

      B: _____

10. (they / finish / packing for the trip / by August 31?

      A: _____

      B: _____

UNIT

NEGATIVE *YES/NO* QUESTIONS AND TAG QUESTIONS

❶ AFFIRMATIVE AND NEGATIVE TAG QUESTIONS AND SHORT ANSWERS

A couple wants to rent an apartment. Complete their questions to the landlord. Provide short answers based on the apartment ad.

> N. Smithfield unfurn. 1 BR in owner occup. bldg.,
> renovated kitchen w. all new appliances, incl. DW,
> near all transp. & shopping, $500/mo. + util., avail.
> for immed. occup. No pets. 555-7738

1. **A:** The rent is $500, __*isn't it?*_____

   B: __*Yes, it is.*_____

2. **A:** The rent includes electricity, _____

   B: _____

3. **A:** It isn't furnished, _____

   B: _____

4. **A:** You've renovated the kitchen, _____

   B: _____

5. **A:** The kitchen doesn't have a dishwasher, _____

   B: _____

6. **A:** You just put in a new refrigerator, _____

   B: _____

35

(continued on next page)

7. **A:** There's a bus nearby, _____

   B: _____

8. **A:** We can't move in right away, _____

   B: _____

9. **A:** You won't allow pets, _____

   B: _____

10. **A:** You live right in the building, _____

    B: _____

2 NEGATIVE QUESTIONS AND SHORT ANSWERS

*Todd is finding out information about two communities. Complete his
conversation with a realtor. Use negative questions to ask about
Greenwood. Use short answers based on the information in the box.*

Greenwood—Community Profile

Greenwood became a town in 1782.

Schools: Greenwood High School, Greenwood Community College

Shopping: Greenwood Mall

Transportation: local public bus

Recreational Facilities: Briar State Park, Greenwood Beach (private),

Davis Baseball Stadium (planned for next year)

Cultural Opportunities: movie theaters (Greenwood Mall)

Average Rent: $678

---

1. **REALTOR:** North Smithfield has a community college.

   TODD: Doesn't Greenwood have a community college? _____

   REALTOR: Yes, it does. _____

2. **REALTOR:** North Smithfield has a public beach.

   TODD: _____

   REALTOR: _____

3. REALTOR: There's an airport in North Smithfield.

TODD: _____

REALTOR: _____

4. REALTOR: You can see live theater in North Smithfield.

TODD: _____

REALTOR: _____

5. REALTOR: People in North Smithfield shop at the mall.

TODD: _____

REALTOR: _____

6. REALTOR: The average rent in North Smithfield is under $700.

TODD: _____

REALTOR: _____

7. REALTOR: North Smithfield has been a town for more than a hundred years.

TODD: _____

REALTOR: _____

8. REALTOR: They're going to build a baseball stadium in North Smithfield.

TODD: _____

REALTOR: _____

❸ NEGATIVE QUESTIONS AND TAG QUESTIONS

Complete these conversations with negative questions and tag questions.
Use the correct form of the verbs in parentheses.

1. A: _____ Didn't _____ you _____ move _____ in last week?
          a. (move)

B: Yes. You haven't been living here very long yourself, _____ have you _____ ?
                                                                              b.

A: Oh, it's been about a year now.

B: It _____ a nice place to live, isn't it?
          c. (be)

A: We think so.

(continued on next page)

2. A: You _____ the letter carrier this morning, have you?
a. (see)

B: No, why?

A: I don't think our mail is being forwarded from our old address.

B: _____ you _____ one of those
b. (fill out)

change-of-address forms?

A: Yes. But that was almost a month ago. Our mail should be coming here by now,

_____?
c.

B: I would think so.

3. A: _____ there an all night supermarket nearby?
a. (be)

B: Yes. It's at 10th and Walnut.

A: Oh. I know where that is. _____ there

_____ a restaurant there?
b. (used to / be)

B: That's right. It closed down last year.

A: That's strange. It _____ there very long, had it?
c. (be)

B: Just about a year. The location just wasn't good for a restaurant.

4. A: The new neighbors are really friendly, _____?
a.

B: Yes. That reminds me. The people across the hall invited us over for coffee and cake

on Saturday. You haven't made any plans for then, _____?
b.

A: Well, I was going to work on our taxes.

B: _____ you _____ a little break?
c. (can / take)

A: Sure. Why not?

4 NEGATIVE QUESTIONS AND TAG QUESTIONS

The new tenants are going to visit their neighbors. They want to confirm some of the assumptions they have. Rewrite their ideas. Use negative questions or tag questions. For some sentences both types of questions are possible. Remember: The only time you can use negative questions is when you think the answer is Yes.

1. We think the people in apartment 4F have lived here a long time.

The people in apartment 4F have lived here a long time, haven't they?

OR

Haven't the people in apartment 4F lived here a long time?

2. I don't think our apartment had been occupied for a while.

Our apartment hadn't been occupied for a while, had it?

3. We believe this is a good building.

_____

4. It seems that the owner takes good care of it.

_____

5. It looks like he recently redid the lobby.

_____

6. I have the impression he doesn't talk very much.

_____

7. I don't think the rent will increase next year.

_____

8. We don't think that there are many vacant apartments.

_____

9. It looks like some new people will be moving into apartment 1B.

_____

10. We have the impression that this is really a nice place to live.

_____

8 ADDITIONS AND RESPONSES WITH *SO, TOO, NEITHER, NOT EITHER,* AND *BUT*

① AFFIRMATIVE OR NEGATIVE

Complete the additions and responses in the following article. Choose between affirmative and negative forms.

Bringing Up Baby

by Rosa Canina

Alana Diller has a lot in common with her neighbor Haley Brown. Alana works full time, and _____ *so* _____ does Haley.
                                                           1.
Alana has just hired a sitter for her baby. Haley

_____ too. And they're both careful parents. Alana
            2.
interviewed a lot of people before deciding on the best person for the

job. So _____ Haley.
              3.

There's one important difference, however. Alana's Brendan is a

human baby, _____ Haley's Agnes isn't. Agnes is a
                        4.
Great Dane, a dog the size of a small pony.

Haley says, "I feel very responsible for Agnes. It's like having a

child. Alana can't leave her baby alone for ten hours every day, and

_____ can I. Both Brendan and Agnes need human
         5.
contact and care during the day."

Jack Austin, owner of PetCare, agrees. "Human children are social

---

creatures, and so _____ pets, especially dogs. Being alone is painful

    6.

for them and bad for their health too."

   "Most of us think of our pets as our babies," continued Austin. "My friends who

are parents don't mind buying the best food for their babies, and I don't

_____. They want their kids to go to the best schools, and so

          7.

_____ I."

       8.

   Schools? Aren't we carrying this comparison a little too far? "Not at all," says

Austin. "Our puppy kindergarten performs the same service for dogs that a human

kindergarten does for children. A five-year-old child will need to learn about his or her

environment, and so _____ a puppy. A child will need to develop

               9.

social skills, and a puppy will _____." Austin's company even offers

                10.

play dates so that shy dogs can make new friends.

   "A lot of my friends think it's silly," laughed Haley, "but I _____. I

                               11.

have my social contacts, and _____ does Agnes. The peace of mind is

              12.

worth the expense."

2 AFFIRMATIVE OR NEGATIVE

Complete the conversation with additions and responses. Choose
between affirmative and negative forms.

A: How did you and Roger meet?

B: Well, I own a dog, and _____ *so does* _____ Roger. My dog, Agnes,

                    1.

   and I used to walk in the park every morning, and Roger and Booboo

   _____.

       2.

A: So you got to know each other walking your dogs?

(continued on next page)

B: Yep. Agnes doesn't like her leash, and _____ Booboo. One

                   3.

morning they were both walking off the leash. Agnes started chasing a squirrel, and

_____ Booboo.

          4.

A: The same squirrel?

B: Right. Roger caught Booboo, but I couldn't catch Agnes. And Roger

_____. She's huge, you know. She ran right out of sight.

        5.

A: What did you do?

B: Well, I wanted to give up and call the police, _____ Roger _____.

                                                   6.

He kept on looking for her while I held Booboo.

A: So you invited him to dinner and found out that you had a lot in common.

B: Right. I'm crazy about dogs, and _____ Roger. In fact, I've

                        7.

never been without one, and he _____.

                        8.

A: What do the two of you have in common besides your love of animals?

B: Oh! Where should I begin? I love hiking. _____ Roger.

                              9.

I can't stand watching TV. _____ he. I've been thinking

                    10.

about learning how to skydive. _____ he.

                    11.

A: Don't you two disagree about anything?

B: Sure. Lots of things. He wants to move out of the city, _____ I

_____. I love it here.

   12.

3 AFFIRMATIVE OR NEGATIVE

Look at the requirements of various pets. Then complete the sentences below with appropriate additions and responses about the pets mentioned in parentheses.

Choosing the Right Pet				
	Dogs	**Cats**	**Birds**	**Fish**
Housing	need bed	need bed	need cage	need aquarium
Food	once a day	twice a day	food always available	once or twice a day; remove uneaten food
Care and Grooming	more than 1 hour a day; need grooming	1/2 hour a day; need grooming	1/2 hour a day; no grooming	1 hour a week; no grooming
Company and Attention Your Pet Needs from You	a lot	a medium amount	a medium amount	none
Life Span	10 years or more	10 years or more	canaries: 5–10 years parrots: 60 years or more	2–10 years
Veterinary Care	yearly visits	yearly visits	when sick	when sick
Expense	medium	medium	low	low

(continued on next page)

1. Dogs need their own bed, _____ and so do cats _____ .
      <u>(cats)</u>

2. Birds should have food available at all times, _____ .
                                          <u>(fish)</u>

3. Cats must have specific mealtimes, _____ .
                                <u>(dogs)</u>

4. Birds don't require a lot of time for care, _____ .
                                      <u>(fish)</u>

5. Dogs and cats need grooming, _____ .
                        <u>(birds and fish)</u>

6. A dog needs a lot of companionship, _____ .
                              <u>(a fish)</u>

7. A bird can get along without much attention, _____ .
                                        <u>(a fish)</u>

8. Dogs and cats will live at least ten years, _____ .
                                    <u>(some fish)</u>

9. Parrots have a life span of more than sixty years, _____ .
                                            <u>(other pets)</u>

10. Birds don't need to see the vet regularly, _____ .
                                    <u>(fish)</u>

11. Dogs have to have a checkup every year, _____ .
                                  <u>(cats)</u>

12. Fish don't cost much to keep, _____ .
                        <u>(birds)</u>

GERUNDS AND INFINITIVES: REVIEW AND EXPANSION

1 GERUND OR INFINITIVE

Write the verbs from the box in the correct column.
Note: Some verbs will go in both columns.

want	enjoy	forget	stop	practice	prepare
offer	need	recommend	quit	dislike	avoid
love	remember	hate	consider	decide	learn
promise	prefer	seem	give up	manage	feel like

Verb + Gerund	Verb + Infinitive
	want

❷ GERUND OR INFINITIVE

Complete this article with the correct form of the verbs in parentheses.
Choose between gerunds and infinitives.

Too Angry <u>TO REMEMBER</u> the Commercials?
1. (remember)

According to a new study, _____ violent TV shows makes it difficult
2. (watch)
_____ brand names or commercial messages. Violence creates anger,
3. (recall)
and instead of _____ the commercials, viewers are attempting _____
4. (hear)   **5. (calm)**
themselves down after violent scenes. The conclusion: _____ violent
6. (sponsor)
programs may not be profitable for advertisers.

This conclusion is good news for the parents, teachers, and lawmakers who are

struggling _____ the amount of violence on U.S. television. They had a
7. (limit)
small victory in 1997, when lawmakers and the television industry designed a TV

ratings system. Unfortunately, Congress did not ask parents _____
8. (participate)
in _____ the system, and the industry does not invite parents
9. (create)
_____ shows before it assigns ratings. As a result, parents are still
10. (preview)
guessing about the content of the shows their kids watch.

Why are we worrying about _____ television violence? The numbers tell
11. (reduce)
the story: A typical child will see 8,000 murders and 100,000 acts of violence between

the ages of three and twelve! It's impossible _____ that this input won't
12. (believe)
affect young children. In fact, researchers have noted three possible effects of

_____ this much violence:
13. (view)
    1. Children may become less sensitive to other people's suffering.

    2. They may also become fearful of _____ with other people.
                                            14. (interact)
    3. They may be more likely _____ in a way that's harmful to others.
                                15. (behave)

Studies show that a huge majority of people want commercial TV _____

16. (produce)

more educational and informational programs. More than 75% believe in

_____ the number of hours of TV that children watch. And the American

17. (limit)

Academy of Pediatrics recommends _____ children _____ more

18. (not permit)   **19. (watch)**

than one to two hours per day.

It's hard _____ why the entertainment industry resists _____

20. (understand)   **21. (make)**

changes. Parents, teachers, and doctors are urging the industry _____

22. (develop)

clearer ratings and _____ violence in children's shows. In addition, violence

23. (get rid of)

seems _____ money for advertisers. Even artists in the industry are

24. (not make)

warning the industry _____ _____ change.

25. (not continue)   **26. (avoid)**

The industry may choose _____ attention to the public, but it will not be

27. (not pay)

able to ignore Congress. Lawmakers want _____ the way networks market

28. (investigate)

violent shows to teenagers. They are also asking the industry _____

29. (offer)

violence-free hours, when no violent content is allowed. Hopefully, parents in the United

States will someday feel good about their children _____ the family TV.

30. (turn on)

❸ GERUND OR INFINITIVE

Complete this interview with a doctor about children and TV violence.
Use the words in the box and the correct form of the verbs in
parentheses. Choose between gerunds and infinitives.

~~shocked~~ likely   fed up with   used to   unwilling

A: I was ___shocked___ ___to learn___ that children will see 100,000 acts of violence

1. (learn)

on television before they are twelve. I had no idea it was that bad.

B: Yes, that is an alarming statistic.

A: It also appears that the networks are _____ _____. They seem

2. (change)

pretty satisfied with things the way they are.

B: Yes, I think that they're _____ _____ all the responsibility on the

3. (put)

viewer. That's the way it's always been, and they're accustomed to it.

(continued on next page)

A: The networks may not want to change, but I know a lot of us are _____

_____ violence during family viewing times. We're really sick of it. A lot of
    4. (see)
my friends don't even turn on the cartoons anymore.

B: That's probably a good idea. Several studies show that children are more

_____ _____ others after they watch violent cartoons. It's really
    5. (hit)
quite predictable.

decide	dislike	hesitate	stop	force

A: OK. Now what can we do about this problem?

B: Well, viewers can make a big difference. First of all, we have to put a lot of pressure on

the networks and _____ them _____ shows more clearly. They'll
    6. (rate)
give in if enough viewers tell them they must.

A: What else?

B: When you see something you don't like, pick up the phone immediately. Don't wait. We

shouldn't _____ _____ the networks about material that we find
    7. (tell)
offensive. Recently a network _____ _____ a violent ad for another
    8. (run)
show right in the middle of a family sitcom. So many people complained that they

reversed that decision and _____ _____ the ad in that time slot.
    9. (show)
A: Violence bothers my kids, but they _____ _____ a show once it
    10. (turn off)
starts. They want to stick it out to the end.

dream of	forbid	permit	insist on

B: Parents have to assert their authority and _____ _____ the
    11. (change)
channel when violence appears. Sometimes they'll face a lot of resistance, but they

should be firm.

A: You know, in a lot of families, parents work until six. They can't successfully

_____ _____ certain shows. They're just not around to enforce
    12. (turn on)
the rules.

B: Help is here from the electronics industry in the form of a V-chip.

A: What exactly is a V-chip?

B: It's a chip that is built into television sets. The V-chip doesn't _____

_____ violent shows. It blocks them electronically.
    13. (tune in)

A: It sounds like something all parents _____ _____.
                                      14. (own)

agree	advise	hesitate	keep

A: Is there anything else that you _____ parents _____?
                                    15. (do)

B: Parents must _____ _____ with their children. They should not
                  16. (communicate)

_____ _____ their kids about their feelings, opinions, and their
        17. (ask)

activities.

A: Thank you, Doctor, for _____ _____ to us today.
                            18. (speak)

❹ OBJECTS WITH GERUNDS AND INFINITIVES

Read the conversations about watching television. Then write summary statements.

1. **KIDS:** Can we watch "Biker Mice from Mars," Mom? Please? Just this once?

   MOM: I'm sorry, but it's just too violent. How about "Beakman's World"?

   SUMMARY: ___The mother didn't allow them to watch it.___
           (the mother / allow / they /watch it)

2. **ANNIE:** Our parents just bought a V-chip.

   BEA: What's that?

   ANNIE: It's something that blocks violent shows so that we can't watch them.

   SUMMARY: _____
           (a V-chip / interfere with / they / watch violent shows)

3. **ROGER:** Beakman really wants viewers to send in science questions.

   CORA: I know. He keeps on telling them that their questions are great.

   SUMMARY: _____
           (Beakman / encourage / they / send in questions)

(continued on next page)

4.   **DAD:** You were having some pretty bad nightmares last night, Jennifer. I think

you'd better stop watching those cop shows.

JENNIFER: OK, but I really love them.

SUMMARY: _____
(the father / object to / Jennifer / watch cop shows)

5. STUDENTS: We want to watch the TV news, but the reporting on adult news shows is

really frightening.

TEACHER: Try "Nick News." It won an award for news reporting for kids.

SUMMARY: _____
(the teacher / recommend / they / watch "Nick News")

6.   **SUE:** I'll never forget that great Knicks game we watched last year.

BOB: What Knicks game?

SUE: Don't you remember? We saw it together! The Knicks beat the Rockets 91–85.

SUMMARY: _____
(Bob / remember / they / see that game)

7.   **FRED:** Does Sharif still watch "Z-Men" every Saturday?

ABU: No. We explained that it was too violent for him, and he decided not to

watch it anymore.

SUMMARY: _____
(Sharif's parents / persuade / he / watch "Z-Men")

8.   **MOM:** Sara, it's nine o'clock. Time to turn off the TV.

SARA: Oh, Mom. Just a little longer, OK?

MOM: You know the rules. No TV after nine o'clock.

SUMMARY: _____
(the mother / insist on / Sara / turn off the TV)

9.   **AZIZA:** This is boring. What's on the other channels?

BEN: I don't know. Where's the remote control?

SUMMARY: _____
(Aziza / want / Ben / change the channel)

10.   **NICK:** Wow! This is great!

PAUL: How can you watch this stuff? It's so violent!

SUMMARY: _____
(Paul / can't understand / Nick / watch the show)

⑤ EDITING

Read this student's essay. Find and correct eleven mistakes in the use of gerunds and infinitives. The first mistake is already corrected.

Asoka Jayawardena

English 220

May 30

Violence on TV

              hearing
I'm tired of ~~hear~~ that violence on TV causes violence at home, in school, and on the streets. Almost all young people watch TV, but not all of them are involved in committing crimes! In fact, very few people choose acting in violent ways. To watch TV, therefore, is not the cause.

Groups like the American Medical Society should stop to try to tell people what to watch. If we want living in a free society, it is necessary having freedom of choice. Children need learn values from their parents. It should be the parents' responsibility deciding what their child can or cannot watch. The government and other interest groups should avoid to interfere in these personal decisions. Limiting our freedom of choice is not the answer. If parents teach their children respecting life, children can enjoy to watch TV without any negative effects.

MAKE, HAVE, LET, HELP, AND GET

1 CONTRAST: *MAKE, HAVE, LET, HELP,* AND *GET*

Complete this article about math teacher Jaime Escalante by circling the correct verb.

Recipe for Success

Born in Bolivia, Jaime Escalante emigrated to the United States to follow his passion—teaching mathematics. He taught at Garfield High, an East Los Angeles high school known for its tough students and its drop-out rate of almost 55 percent. The school administration was so weak that they **let** / made gangs of students (and
1.
nonstudents) roam the halls and spray the walls with graffiti.
Escalante changed all that. He let / **made** students do huge
2.
amounts of homework, take daily quizzes, and fill out daily time cards. He believed in his students' ability to succeed and would never **get** / let them drop out of class. He considered vacations a
3.
waste of time and let / **made** his students do homework during the
4.
semester break. He even planned two full mornings of classes during spring vacation. He wasn't going to let / **make** a school
5.
vacation erase what his students had learned!

Escalante often used nontraditional methods. To develop a spirit of camaraderie, he got / had his students
6.
to do football-like cheers before the start of class. He praised them, teased them, insulted them—anything that worked. Most of all, he got / helped
7.
them believe in themselves.

Then Escalante did the impossible. He had / got his students take the Advanced
8.
Placement calculus exam, a national test that only 2 percent of high school students take. This difficult exam gives students college credit for high school work. In preparation for the test, Escalante let / made his class work harder than ever.
9.
Because his students did so well on the test, and because many of them made the same kind of mistake in one of the problems, the testing company suspected them of cheating. To prove their innocence, Escalante decided to get / have them take the
10.
test again. To make sure that no cheating could occur, the official administering the test let / made them sit at desks spaced wide apart. Everyone passed, proving once
11.
and for all that even students from "disadvantaged" backgrounds could succeed.

Escalante's story became well known when film director Ramón Menéndez made the movie *Stand and Deliver.* Escalante got / let the actor Edward James Olmos,
12.
who plays him in the film, spend eighteen hours a day with him. Escalante, as well as movie critics and theater critics, was pleased with the results.

What makes Escalante such an effective teacher? In the words of one of his students, Escalante "really cares. He let / made us feel powerful, that we could do
13.
anything."

2 AFFIRMATIVE AND NEGATIVE STATEMENTS

At the beginning of the semester, Jaime Escalante handed out a list of instructions similar to this. Read the instructions.

SUBJECT GRADE

Tests		*Quizzes*
A	90–100%	7
B	80–89%	6
C	70–79%	5
D	60–69%	4

TESTS (100 points each): All tests will be on *Fridays* and you must take them in class. *No make-up* tests will be given.

QUIZZES (10 points each): Almost every day and must be taken in class; *no make-up* quizzes will be given.

HOMEWORK (10 points each): All homework assignments will be collected. When turned in, the paper should have your name, period, and homeroom number. They must be written in the upper-right corner.

WORK HABITS: No late homework or make-up work will be accepted.

COOPERATION: Five tardies* = U

NOTEBOOK (possible 50 points): Each student will keep a notebook, not a pee-chee folder or any other type of loose file, in which he/she shall keep his/her work composed of two sections:
    i. Class notes (you should take notes carefully in class)
    ii. Quizzes and tests
  On Fridays each student shall submit his/her notebook to the teacher for credit.

ATTENDANCE: You are expected to attend the class daily. If you are absent five (5) times during the semester, you will be referred to the Dean. If you miss three (3) tests during the semester, you may be referred to your counselor.

PLACE THIS PAPER IN YOUR NOTEBOOK
FOR A BETTER EDUCATION

_____   _____
Student's Signature   J.A. Escalante
                                                           Mathematics Teacher

---

* *tardies* = latenesses

(continued on next page)

Use the information from the instructions and complete these sentences about Escalante's class. Choose affirmative or negative.

1. He _____made them take_____ tests every Friday.
   (make / take)
2. He _____ make-up tests.
   (let / take)
3. He _____ quiz questions almost every day.
   (have / answer)
4. He _____ their homework assignments.
   (make / hand in)
5. He _____ their homework late.
   (let / submit)
6. He _____ their names in the upper right corner.
   (have / write)
7. He _____ late four times before giving them a grade of U.
   (let / come)
8. He _____ their notebooks every week.
   (have / submit)
9. He _____ the sheet.
   (make / sign)
10. He _____ a neatly organized notebook.
    (have / keep)
11. He _____ to the dean if they missed three tests.
    (make / go)
12. The purpose of these rules was to _____ well in the course.
    (help / do)

❸ AFFIRMATIVE AND NEGATIVE STATEMENTS

Read these short conversations, which take place in Mrs. Olinski's math class. Complete the summary sentences, using the verbs in parentheses. Choose affirmative or negative.

1. **MARTA:** Can we please take a short break?

   MRS. O.: Sure. We'll break for ten minutes.

   SUMMARY: The teacher _____let them take a break._____
   (let)
2. **MARK:** I can't solve this problem. Can you show me how to do it?

   MRS. O.: It's better if you work it out yourself.

   SUMMARY: She _____
   (make)

(continued on next page)

3.   **SARA:** The answer is 5.34.

   MRS. O.: No. I'll give you one more chance to get it right. Try again.

   SUMMARY: She _____
   (make)

4. **MRS. O.:** Your homework is a mess. I'd like you to do it over.

   ROBERT: Oh, OK.

   SUMMARY: She _____
   (have)

5.   **DELIA:** Can we use our calculators during the trigonometry exam?

   MRS. O.: Absolutely not.

   SUMMARY: She _____
   (let)

6. **MRS. O.:** I would really appreciate it if some of you would help clean up this classroom.

   DAVID: OK. We'll do it.

   SUMMARY: She _____
   (get)

4 EDITING

Read this student's journal entry. Find and correct seven mistakes in the use of **make**, **have**, **let**, **help**, *and* **get**. *The first mistake is already corrected.*

November 11

   Mrs. Olinski made us ~~to~~ stay *late again after class today. She wants to help us*

passing our next test by giving us extra time to review in class. She won't make us

use calculators during the test. She says, "Calculators make students to forget how

to add two plus two!" She's always trying to get us use our brains instead. She has

us solve lots of homework problems, and she gets us asking lots of questions in

class. She's strict, but I think she's a good teacher. She's definitely dedicated. She

even let's us call her at home. She's certainly gotten me to learn more than I ever

did before. Now, if she could only get me to enjoy math, that would really be an

accomplishment!

UNIT

11

PHRASAL VERBS: REVIEW

1 PARTICLES

Complete the phrasal verbs with particles from the box.
You will use some particles more than once.

ahead	back	down	up
on	out	over	

Phrasal Verb	**Meaning**
1. catch _____on_____	*become popular*
2. cheer _____	*make someone feel happier*
3. do _____	*do again*
4. get _____	*make progress, succeed*
5. let _____	*allow to leave*
6. let _____	*disappoint*
7. look _____	*examine*
8. pick _____	*select or identify*
9. take _____	*return*
10. try _____	*use to find out if it works*
11. turn _____	*raise the volume*
12. turn _____	*lower the volume*
13. use _____	*consume*
14. write _____	*write on a piece of paper*

❷ PHRASAL VERBS

*Complete the article. Choose the phrasal verb from the box that is
closest in meaning to the words in parentheses. Use the correct form of
the phrasal verb.*

burn up	cut down	get together	give out		go back	throw away
go out	~~pay back~~	put on		put together	set up	

Starting New

Wearing new clothes, <u>paying back</u> debts, lighting candles—many cultures
    1. (repay)

share similar New Year traditions. In Iran, for example, people celebrate *Now Ruz,*

or New Day, on the first day of spring. A few days before the festival, families

_____ bushes and _____ piles of wood. They set the piles on
2. (bring down by cutting)   **3. (assemble)**

fire, and before the wood _____, each family member jumps over one of
4. (burn completely)

the fires and says, "I give you my pale face, and I take your red one." The day before

the New Year begins, the family _____ a table in the main room with
5. (prepare for use)

special foods and objects, such as colored eggs, cake, and the *haft-sin,* seven objects

with names beginning with the sound "s." Everyone _____ new clothes,
6. (cover the body with)

and the family _____ around the table. When the New Year begins, family
7. (meet)

members hug each other and _____ gifts, especially to the children. For
8. (distribute)

the next twelve days, people visit each other, but on the thirteenth day, it is unlucky

to be inside a house, so people _____ and spend the day in parks and
9. (leave)

fields, where they spend the time having picnics, listening to music, and playing sports.

They don't _____ home until sunset. At the end of the day, every one
10. (return)

"_____" bad luck by throwing wheat or lentils into a river.
11. (discard)

3 PHRASAL VERBS AND PRONOUN OBJECTS

Complete each conversation with phrasal verbs and pronouns.

1. A: We need to pick up two dozen candles for *Diwali.*

   B: I'll _____ pick them up _____ after work.

   A: While you're there, why don't you pick out some new decorations?

   B: Let's have the children _____. You know how excited they

   get about the Hindu New Year.

2. A: It's time for us to empty out our pockets.

   B: Why do you _____?

   A: It's a custom for the Jewish New Year. On *Rosh Hashana,* we throw away the things

   in our pockets. It's like throwing away last year's bad memories.

   B: Here's my cigarette lighter. I'd love to _____.

3. A: When will we set off the firecrackers for the Chinese New Year?

   B: We won't _____ until dark.

   A: How do firecrackers keep away evil spirits?

   B: The noise probably _____.

4. A: Are you hanging up those green streamers for Christmas?

   B: No, we're _____ for Kwanzaa, the African-American

   harvest celebration. It comes at the same time as Christmas and New Year.

   A: What is your mom setting up on the table?

   B: That's a *kinara.* We _____ to hold the Kwanzaa candles.

5. A: Do you usually write down your New Year's resolutions?

   B: Yes. I _____ because they're so easy to forget by

   February.

   A: This year I'd like to give up desserts.

   B: I _____ for a few months last year. I lost five pounds.

4 EDITING

Read this person's list of New Year's resolutions. Find and correct eleven mistakes in the use of phrasal verbs. The first mistake is already corrected.

New Year's Resolutions

Wake ~~out~~ up earlier. (No later than 7:30!)

Work out in the gym at least three times a week.

Lose five pounds. (Give over eating so many desserts.)

Be more conscious of the environment—

—Don't throw down newspapers. Recycle them.

—Save energy. Turn on the lights when I leave the

apartment.

Straighten up my room.

—Hang out my clothes when I take off them.

—Put my books back where they belong.

—Give some of my old books and clothing that I no

longer wear away.

Don't put off doing my homework assignments. Hand in them

on time!

Read more.

Use the dictionary more. (Look over words I don't know.)

When someone calls and leaves a message, call them back

right away. Don't put off it!

Get to know my neighbors. Ask them for coffee over.

Phrasal Verbs:
Separable and Inseparable

 PARTICLES

Complete the phrasal verbs with the correct particles.

	Phrasal Verb		**Definition**
1.	call	back	*return a phone call*
2.	get		*recover from an illness or bad situation*
3.	cross		*draw a line through*
4.	call		*cancel*
5.	drop		*visit unexpectedly*
6.	point		*indicate*
7.	keep		*continue*
8.	talk		*persuade*
9.	blow		*explode*
10.	think		*consider*
11.	throw		*discard*
12.	put		*return to its original place*
13.	work		*solve*

❷ PHRASAL VERBS

It is said that necessity is the mother of invention. Read about some inventors and their clever solutions to everyday problems. Complete the stories with the appropriate form of the correct phrasal verbs from the boxes.

~~call on~~	call up	carry out
catch on	do over	figure out
give up	hand out	set up

1. **Edwin Cox** was a door-to-door salesman. Among the products he sold were aluminum

   pots and pans. However, the homemakers he _____*called on*_____ were not

            a.

   interested in his products, and sometimes they wouldn't

   even let him enter their homes. Cox needed to

   _____ an idea that would get
          b.

   him through the door. He knew that people were

   unhappy with the way food stuck to pans. If only he

   could find a way to combine the strength of steel wool

   and the cleaning power of soap, he might solve both their problem and his. Cox

   designed and _____ some experiments in his own kitchen.
             c.

   He dipped small, square steel-wool pads into a soapy solution and then dried them. He

   _____ this _____ again and again
                  d.

   until the pad was totally filled with dried soap. He _____ the
                          e.

   soap pads as free samples—just one to a customer. The pads _____,
                                       f.

   and soon people were _____ him _____
                                                g.

   to ask where they could buy more. Within a few months, Cox was able to

   _____ his door-to-door trade, and, in 1917, he
              h.

   _____ a business to produce the S.O.S.® soap pad.
              i.

bring out	catch on	come up with
end up	find out	grow up
push up	put together	turn on

2. Josephine Cochrane decided, in 1886, to invent a dishwashing machine. Although she

had _____ in a wealthy family and had never washed a dish
　　　　　　　　a.

in her life, she was upset by the number of dishes broken by her household staff. Every

dinner party _____ with shattered china that took months to
　　　　　　　　b.

replace. Cochrane _____ her machine in a woodshed
　　　　　　　　c.

attached to her home. The machine was made up of wire compartments for plates,

saucers, and cups. The compartments were attached to a wheel that was in a large

boiler. When she _____ the
　　　　　　　　d.

motor, the wheel turned and _____
　　　　　　　　e.

soapy water from the bottom of the boiler. The water

then "rained down" on the dishes. When hotels and

restaurants _____ about her
　　　　　　　　f.

invention, they started placing orders. Cochrane realized

that she had _____ a valuable
　　　　　　　　g.

machine and she patented her invention. About thirty

years later, her company _____ a smaller model for the
　　　　　　　　h.

average home, but it wasn't until the 1950s, when more women began working outside

the home, that the dishwasher really _____.
　　　　　　　　i.

Source: Charles Panati, *Extraordinary Origins of Everyday Things.* New York: Harper & Row, 1987.

❸ PHRASAL VERBS AND OBJECT PRONOUNS

Complete the conversations. Use phrasal verbs and pronouns.

1. **Luis:** I thought you were going to ask the Riveras over for dinner.

   Ines: I did. I _____asked them over_____ for Friday night.

2. **Luis:** Did you invite their son, too? He gets along well with Jimmy.

   Ines: That's a good idea. He really does _____.

3. **Ines:** If you run into Marta tomorrow, invite her too. She knows the Riveras.

   Luis: I usually don't _____ on Tuesdays. If we want her

   to come, we should call.

4. **Ines:** I'd like you to straighten up your room before the Riveras come over.

   Jimmy: No problem. I'll _____ as soon as I come home

   from school Friday.

5. **Jimmy:** What time do you think we'll get through with dinner? There's a really good

   movie on TV at nine o'clock.

   Ines: I don't know what time we'll get through with dinner. But even if we

   _____ early, I don't think it's appropriate to turn on

   the TV while we have guests, do you?

6. **Ines:** Maybe you could pick out some CDs to play during dinner.

   Jimmy: Sure. I'll _____ right now.

7. **Ines:** I hope we don't run out of eggs and milk.

   Jimmy: Don't worry about milk. If we _____, I can always

   get some at the A & W.

8. **INES:** You can bring out the roast now. It's done.

    LUIS: Great. I'll _____ right away so we can eat. It smells great.

9. **INES:** Be careful! Don't pick up the pan without pot holders! It's hot!

    LUIS: Ow! Too late! I already _____.

10. **LUIS:** I'm going to turn down the music. It's a little too loud.

    INES: Oh, don't get up. I'll _____.

11. **LUIS:** Should I cover up the leftovers?

    INES: Uh-huh. Here's some aluminum foil. After you _____, you can put them in the refrigerator.

12. **LUIS:** Oh, no. I've used up the soap pads.

    INES: You haven't _____. There's another whole box under the sink.

13. **INES:** Could you help me put away the dishes?

    LUIS: Why don't you rest? I'll _____ for you.

14. **INES:** Don't forget to turn on the dishwasher before you go to bed.

    LUIS: I'll _____ now. That way I won't forget.

15. **INES:** Good night. I'm going to bed and try to figure out that crossword puzzle that's been giving me trouble.

    LUIS: Good luck! Let me know if you _____.

4 DEFINITIONS

See if you can figure out this puzzle.

ACROSS

4. Gets off (the bus)
7. Want
11. Mix up
13. Figure out
16. Opposite of *fall*
17. Leave out

DOWN

1. Pick _____ up at 5:00.
   I'll be ready then.
2. Hello
3. You and I
4. Pick up
5. Advertisements *(short form)*

ACROSS

18. Think up
19. These can run out of ink.
21. _____ it rains, it pours.
23. Call up
25. Don't go away. Please _____.
26. Street *(short form)*
27. Middle
31. Call off
32. Indefinite article
33. Professional *(short form)*
34. Maryland *(short form)*
36. What time _____ she usually show up?
38. Negative word
40. Take place
41. Put up (a building)

DOWN

6. Hands in
7. Talk over
8. Tell off
9. Take back
10. Carry on
12. Look over
14. *am, is,* _____
15. Eastern Standard Time *(short form)*
18. Drop _____ on
19. Put off
20. Come in
21. The music is loud. Please turn _____ down.
22. Pass out
24. Blow up
27. Her book _____ out last year.
28. Ends up
29. Rte.
30. Call on
31. You put a Band-Aid® on it.
35. Don't guess. Look it _____.
37. Please go _____. Don't stop.
39. Either . . . _____.

UNIT

ADJECTIVE CLAUSES WITH SUBJECT RELATIVE PRONOUNS

1 RELATIVE PRONOUNS

In many countries, people sometimes try to meet others through personal ads in magazines and newspapers. Complete these ads by circling the correct relative pronouns.

Best Friends—I'm a 28-year-old man who / which enjoys
1.
reading, baseball, movies, and long walks in the country. You're a
20- to 30-year-old woman who / whose interests are compatible
2.
with mine and who / whose believes that friendship is the basis
3.
of a good marriage. **7932**

Star Struck—You remind me of Kevin Costner, who / that
4.
is my favorite actor. I remind you of a movie who / that is fun
5.
and full of surprises. Won't you be my leading man as we dance
across the screen of life? **3234** ☎

Where Are You?—35-year-old, career-oriented female
who / which relaxes at the gym and who / whose personality
6.   7.
varies from philosophical to funny, seeks male counterpart.
9534 ✍☎

Forever—Are you looking for a relationship who / which will
8.
stand the test of time? Call this 28-year-old male who / which
9.
believes in forever. **2312** ☎

Soulmates?—The things <u>that / who</u> make me happy are
10.
chocolate cake, travel, animals, music, and you, <u>whose / who</u>
11.
ideas of a good time are similar to mine. **1294** ✍🏻

Enough Said—I want to meet a guy <u>who / whose</u> is smart
12.
enough to read, active enough to run for a bus <u>that / who</u> just
13.
left the stop, silly enough to appreciate David Letterman, and
mature enough to want a commitment. I'm a 25-year-old female
<u>who / which</u> finds meaning in building a relationship and family.
6533 ✍🏻
14.

❷ SUBJECT–VERB AGREEMENT

*What are the ingredients of a happy marriage? Read the results of a
study and complete the sentences with appropriate relative pronouns
and the correct form of the verbs in parentheses.*

1. **Ability to Change and Accept Change**

    Successful couples are those _____*who*_____ _____*are*_____ able to adapt to
                                        a.   **b. (be)**

    changes _____ _____ within the marriage or in the other
              c.   **d. (occur)**

    partner. People _____ _____ happily married see themselves "as
                  e.   **f. (stay)**

    free agents _____ _____ choices in life."
                g.   **h. (make)**

2. **Ability to Live with the Unchangeable**

    They can live with situations _____ _____. They accept the
                    a.   **b. (not change)**

    knowledge that there are some conflicts _____ _____
                                c.   **d. (remain)**

    unsolvable. This attitude relates to life in general. According to the study, "People

    _____ marriages _____ because of a crisis, such as an illness or
        e.   **f. (end)**

    a financial disaster, often are people _____ cannot live with the realities of
                                            g.

    their existence." Their only answer is to end the relationship.

(continued on next page)

3. Assumption of "Forever"

Most newlyweds believe their marriage is "forever." This is

an important belief _____ _____ the
                               a.   b. (help)

relationship survive problems.

4. Trust

In marriage, trust allows for the sense of security _____ _____
                                             a.   b. (make)

long and satisfying relationships possible. It is the glue _____
                                                           c.

_____ the marriage together.
        d. (hold)

5. Enjoying Each Other's Company

According to the study, "Although they may spend evenings quietly together in a

room, the silence _____ _____ them is the comfortable silence
                              a.   b. (surround)

of two people _____ _____ they do not have to talk to feel
                        c.   d. (know)

close." They can simply enjoy being together.

6. Shared History

A marriage is a relationship _____ _____ a reality and history
                                 a.   b. (have)

of its own. People in good marriages value their shared history and gain strength

from it. They keep it alive with family stories and photos.

7. Luck

What role does luck play? You need luck in choosing a partner _____
                                                                      a.

_____ the ability to change and trust and love. You need luck, too, in the
     b. (have)

type of family you come from. Research suggests that families _____
                                                            c.

members _____ warm and supportive provide good preparation for
              d. (be)

future relationships. You also need luck with life itself. This is often a question of

attitude. According to the study, "Couples _____ _____
                                            e.   f. (consider)

themselves lucky are the ones _____ _____ luck where they are
                                     g.   h. (seize)

able to." They don't wait for luck to come to them.

Source: Francine Klagsbrun, *Married People: Staying Together in the Age of Divorce.* New York: Bantam Books, 1985.

❸ SENTENCE COMBINING

Combine these pairs of sentences using adjective clauses. Use commas when necessary.

1. I met Rebecca in 1994. Rebecca is now my wife.

   I met Rebecca, who is now my wife, in 1994.

2. She was visiting her aunt. Her aunt's apartment was right across from mine.

3. I loved Rebecca's smile. Her smile was full of warmth and good humor.

4. We shared a lot of interests. The interests brought us close together.

5. We both enjoyed ballroom dancing. Ballroom dancing was very popular then.

6. We also enjoyed playing cards with some of our friends. Our friends lived in the neighborhood.

7. Our friend Mike taught us how to ski. Mike was a professional skier.

8. We got married in a ski lodge. The ski lodge was in Vermont.

9. Our marriage has grown through the years. Our marriage means a lot to us both.

10. We have two children. The children are both in school.

11. We both have jobs. The jobs are important to us.

12. I really love Rebecca. Rebecca is not only my wife but also my best friend.

UNIT

14 ADJECTIVE CLAUSES WITH OBJECT RELATIVE PRONOUNS OR *WHEN* AND *WHERE*

---

1 RELATIVE PRONOUNS AND *WHEN* AND *WHERE*: SUBJECT AND OBJECT

Complete these book dedications and acknowledgments by circling the correct words.

1.

> To my family, which / that has given me my first world, and to
> a.
> my friends, <u>who / whom</u> have taught me how to appreciate the
> b.
> New World after all.

(Eva Hoffman, *Lost in Translation: A Life in a New Language.* New York: Penguin, 1989).

2.

> I'd like to thank everyone <u>which / who</u> has been in my
> a.
> life. But since I can't, I'll single out a few <u>who / whose</u>
> b.
> were particularly helpful to me in the writing of this
> book . . . thanks to my loving and amazingly patient
> wife, Dianne, to all our friends <u>whom / which</u> we
> c.
> couldn't see while I was mired in self-examination,
> and to my family.

(Ben Fong-Torres, *The Rice Room.* New York: Hyperion, 1994.)

72

3.

> My book would not have been written without the encouragement and collaboration of many
>
> people. I should like to thank my wife, <u>who / that</u> has seen little of me at home during the last
>   **a.**
> few years, for her understanding. . . . I should like to thank the NASA personnel at Houston,
>
> Cape Kennedy, and Huntsville, <u>which / who</u> showed me around their magnificent scientific
>   **b.**
> and technical research centers . . . all the countless men and women around the globe
>
> <u>whose / whom</u> practical help, encouragement, and conversation made this book possible.
>   **c.**

(Erich Von Däniken, *Chariots of the Gods?* New York: G.P. Putnam, 1977.)

4.

> *I* ask the indulgence of the children <u>who / whose</u> may read this book for
>   **a.**
> dedicating it to a grown-up. I have a serious reason: he is the best friend I have in the
>
> world. I have another reason: this grown-up understands everything, even books
>
> about children. I have a third reason: he lives in France, <u>which / where</u> he is hungry
>   **b.**
> and cold. He needs cheering up. If all these reasons are not enough, I will dedicate
>
> this book to the child from <u>whom / who</u> this grown-up grew. All grown-ups were once
>   **c.**
> children—although few of them remember it.

(Antoine de Saint-Exupéry, *The Little Prince.* New York: Harcourt Brace, 1943.)

5.

> *The field-work on <u>which / that</u> this book is based covers a span of fourteen years,*
>   **a.**
> *1925–1939; the thinking covers the whole of my professional life, 1923–1948. . . . It is*
>
> *impossible to make articulate . . . the debt I owe to those hundreds of people of the*
>
> *Pacific Islands <u>who / whose</u> patience, tolerance of differences, faith in my goodwill, and*
>   **b.**
> *eager curiosity made these studies possible. Many of the children <u>whom / which</u> I held in*
>   **c.**
> *my arms and from <u>whom / whose</u> tense or relaxed behavior I learned lessons <u>who / that</u>*
>   **d.**   **e.**
> *could have been learned in no other way are now grown men and women; the life they*
>
> *live in the records of an anthropologist must always have about it a quality of wonder*
>
> *both to the anthropologist and to themselves. . . .*

(Margaret Mead, *Male and Female.* New York: William Morrow, 1949.)

(continued on next page)

6.

Nearly every person interviewed for this book has been given relevant portions of the manuscript to check for errors, but any mistakes remain my responsibility. Conversations and events <u>who / that</u> I did not hear or see have been reported as the

a.

participants remembered them. . . . Much has been written about the decline of American education. It is a joy to describe one place <u>where / when</u> that shaky institution

b.

has experienced an unmistakable revival. . . . I hope this book will impart some of that excitement to any <u>which / who</u> wish to set forth in the same direction as Jaime

c.

Escalante and the many other teachers in America like him.

(Jay Mathews, *Escalante: The Best Teacher in America.* New York: Henry Holt, 1988.)

7.

. . . some contributions to my work come from people I have never met and probably never will. I am grateful . . . to the citizens of the city of Portland and the county of Multnomah, Oregon, <u>which / whose</u> taxes support the Multnomah County Library,

a.

without <u>whom / whose</u> reference material this book would not have been written. I am

b.

also grateful to the archaeologists, anthropologists, and other specialists <u>who / whom</u>

c.

wrote the books from <u>which / that</u> I gathered most of this information for the setting

d.

and background of this novel. . . . There are many who helped more directly . . . Karen Auel, <u>that / who</u> encouraged her mother more than she ever knew . . . Cathy

e.

Humble, of <u>which / whom</u> I asked the greatest favor one can ask of a friend—honest

f.

criticism—because I valued her sense of words.

(Jean M. Auel, *The Clan of the Cave Bear.* New York: Crown, 1980.)

② RELATIVE PRONOUNS AND *WHEN* AND *WHERE*: OBJECT

*Complete the article about book dedications and acknowledgments. Use an appropriate relative pronoun, **when**, or **where**, and the correct form of the verb in parentheses.*

To L. F., without _____whose_____ *encouragement . . .*
1.

Dedication and acknowledgment pages are the places _____ an author
                                                           2.

_____ the people _____ assistance he or she _____
3. (thank)   4.   5. (find)

valuable while writing. These words of gratitude are probably the last ones

_____ the author _____ for a book, but they'll be the first ones
6.   7. (write)

_____ a reader _____. This fact may explain some of the problems
8.   9. (read)

_____ writers _____ when writing these pages. The thanks should be
10.   11. (face)

gracious and well written, but the task of writing them comes at the end of a long

project—a time _____ an author sometimes _____ of words.
                12.   13. (run out)

In the sixteenth and seventeenth centuries, _____ rich nobles
                                             14.

_____ artists, writers were paid well for writing dedications in _____
15. (support)   16.

they _____ their wealthy employers. Some "authors" made a profession of
     17. (praise)

dedication writing. They traveled the countryside with fake books into _____
                                                                        18.

they _____ a new dedication at each rich family's house.
     19. (insert)

A modern writer usually dedicates a book to a family member, friend, or colleague with

_____ he or she _____ deeply connected. The dedication page is
20.   21. (feel)

short and often contains only initials of the person to _____ the author
                                                        22.

_____ the work. In the acknowledgments, _____ the author
23. (dedicate)   24.

_____ more room, everyone from reference librarians to proofreaders is
25. (have)

thanked.

Most writers' handbooks give authors very little help with dedications and

acknowledgments. "It's just something _____ you _____ know how
                                       26.   27. (be supposed to)

to handle," complains one author.

3 RELATIVE PRONOUNS, *WHERE*, AND *WHEN*

Combine each pair of sentences, using an appropriate relative pronoun, **where**, *or* **when**. *Use commas when necessary.*

1. Jean M. Auel wrote a novel. I enjoyed reading it.

   Jean M. Auel wrote a novel which I enjoyed reading.

2. *The Clan of the Cave Bear* tells the story of a clan of prehistoric people. Auel started researching the book in 1977.

   _____

3. The clan lived during the Ice Age. Glaciers covered large parts of the earth then.

   _____

4. The story takes place during a period in the Ice Age. The climate was slightly warmer then.

   _____

5. The people lived near the shores of the Black Sea. There are a lot of large caves there.

   _____

6. Bears lived in some of the caves. The clan worshiped bears.

   _____

7. The clan made their home in a large cave. Bears had lived in the cave.

   _____

8. One aspect of their lives is their technical skill. Auel describes that aspect well.

   _____

9. She learned some of the arts. Prehistoric people had practiced them.

   _____

10. In her preface, she thanks a man. She studied the art of making stone tools with him.

    _____

11. She also thanks an Arctic survival expert. She met him while she was doing research.

    _____

12. He taught her to make a snow cave on Mt. Hood. She spent one January night there.

_____

13. She went through a difficult time. She couldn't write then.

_____

14. A fiction writer inspired her to finish her book. She attended the writer's lecture.

_____

15. *The Clan of the Cave Bear* was a best-seller for a long time. Auel published it in 1980.

_____

4 OPTIONAL DELETIONS OF RELATIVE PRONOUNS

In five of the sentences in Exercise 3, the relative pronoun can be deleted. Write the sentences below with the relative pronoun deleted.

1. Jean M. Auel wrote a novel I enjoyed reading. _____

2. _____

3. _____

4. _____

5. _____

5 EDITING

Read this student book report. Find and correct nine mistakes in the use of adjective clauses. The first mistake is already corrected.

For my book report, I read *The Clan of the Cave Bear* by Jean M. Auel. This
novel, ~~that~~ which is about the life of prehistoric people, took years to research. The main character is Ayla. She is found by a wandering clan after an earthquake kills her family. The same earthquake had destroyed the cave in which this clan had lived, and they are searching for another home. The clan leader wants to leave Ayla to die. She is an Other—a human which language and culture his clan doesn't understand. However, the leader's sister Iza, whose Ayla soon calls Mother, adopts her.

The story takes place at a time where human beings are still evolving. Ayla is a new kind of human. Her brain, that she can use to predict and make plans, is different from Iza's and other clan members'. Their brains are adapted to memory, not new learning, whom they fear and distrust. At first, Ayla brings luck to the clan. She accidentally wanders into a place where they find a large cave, perfect for their new home. She is educated by Iza, who's great knowledge everyone respects. The skills that Iza passes on to Ayla include healing and magic, as well as finding food, cooking, and sewing. However, Ayla's powers make it impossible for her to stay with the clan. She learns to hunt, a skill where women are forbidden to practice. Her uncle, that she loves very much, allows her to stay with the clan, but after he dies, she loses his protection. Another earthquake, for which she is blamed, destroys the clan's home, and she is forced to leave.

ANSWER KEY

In this answer key, where the contracted form is given, the full form is also correct, and where the full form is given, the contracted form is also correct.

PART | **PRESENT AND PAST: REVIEW AND EXPANSION**

UNIT **SIMPLE PRESENT TENSE AND PRESENT PROGRESSIVE**

2. ask, asking
3. begin, begins
4. bites, biting
5. buys, buying
6. come, comes
7. digs, digging
8. do, doing
9. employ, employs
10. fly, flies
11. forgets, forgetting
12. have, having
13. lie, lies
14. manages, managing
15. promise, promises
16. say, saying
17. studies, studying
18. travel, travels
19. uses, using
20. write, writing

2

1. b. Are . . . taking
   c. is studying
   d. 's
   e. remember
   f. look
2. a. Do . . . know
   b. 's taking
   c. does . . . mean
   d. don't know
3. a. do . . . spell
   b. have
   c. looks

4. a. are . . . doing
   b. seem
   c. 'm trying
   d. is
   e. types
5. a. Do . . . want
   b. does . . . do
   c. analyzes
   d. write
   e. sign
6. a. are . . . doing
   b. 'm writing
   c. 'm reading
   d. think

3

2. doesn't know
3. is thinking
4. is writing
5. looks
6. studies
7. believe
8. tells
9. are using OR use
10. does . . . hope OR is . . . hoping
11. look
12. tells
13. Does . . . lean
14. indicates
15. represents
16. is planning
17. doesn't leave
18. avoids
19. show
20. 're reading
21. is investigating
22. thinks
23. takes
24. warns
25. doesn't guarantee

❹

Justin—I hope you ~~don't~~ **aren't** feeling angry at me

about my last e-mail. Remember that I wrote,

"I ~~not~~ **don't** want to hear from you again! ':-)" That little

symbol at the end means, "I'm winking, and

I ~~only joke~~ **'m only joking**." We ~~using~~ **use OR are using** a lot of these symbols in

e-mail. We ~~are calling~~ **call** them emoticons because

they show how we are feeling at the moment.

Here are some more:

:-)   I ~~smile~~ **'m smiling**.

:-D   I'm laughing.

:-(I'm frowning.

8-]   Wow! I **'m** really surprised!

(:: ( ) ::)   This ~~is meaning~~ **means**, "I want to help." It

          looks like a Band-Aid.

:-C   I'~~m not believing~~ **don't believe** that!

Please write back soon and tell me that ~~your~~ **you're** not

angry. ((((Justin)))) Those are hugs! Delia

UNIT 2 **SIMPLE PAST TENSE AND PAST PROGRESSIVE**

❶

2. apply
3. was OR were
4. became
5. developed
6. eat
7. feel
8. got
9. grew
10. lived
11. meet
12. pay
13. permitted
14. planned
15. said
16. send
17. slept
18. understood

❷

2. met
3. asked
4. Was
5. did . . . hate
6. Were . . . going to marry OR Did . . . marry
7. found
8. didn't fall
9. were working
10. met

11. hired
12. was trying
13. was
14. was feeling OR felt
15. was pretending OR pretended
16. thought
17. wanted
18. was working
19. came
20. wasn't going to ask
21. solved
22. stopped
23. fell
24. were taking
25. met
26. became
27. was dating
28. didn't seem
29. heard
30. was whispering
31. had to
32. was going to complain
33. changed
34. wasn't
35. didn't stop
36. broke up
37. asked
38. was moving
39. saw
40. was sitting
41. was parking
42. jumped
43. thought
44. was going to ask
45. was helping
46. looked
47. didn't give up
48. ran into
49. introduced
50. invited

❸

I'm really glad that I ~~was deciding~~ **decided** to rent this

apartment. I ~~won't~~ **wasn't going to** move here because the rent is

a little high, but I'm happy I did. All the others

~~were seeming~~ **seemed** so small, and the neighborhoods

just weren't as beautiful as this one. And moving

wasn't as bad as I feared. I was planning to take

more days off work, but then Hakim ~~offers~~ **offered** to

help. What a great brother! We ~~were moving~~ **moved**

everything into the apartment in two days. The

man next door seemed really nice. On the second

day, he even ~~help~~ **helped** Hakim with some of the heavy

furniture. His name is Jared. I ~~don't~~ **didn't** even unpack

the kitchen stuff last weekend because I was so

tired. Last night I ~~walking~~ **walked** Mitzi for only two

blocks. Jared was standing downstairs and ~~looked~~ **(was) looking**

at his mail when I came back. I was going to

~~asked~~ **ask** him over for dinner this weekend (in order

to thank him), but everything is still in boxes.

Maybe in a couple of weeks . . .

UNIT 3 PRESENT PERFECT, PRESENT PERFECT PROGRESSIVE, AND SIMPLE PAST TENSE

2. brought, brought
3. chose, chosen
4. delayed, delayed
5. felt, felt
6. found, found
7. finished, finished
8. got, gotten
9. graduated, graduated
10. hid, hidden
11. moved, moved
12. noticed, noticed
13. owned, owned
14. read, read
15. replied, replied
16. ripped, ripped
17. showed, shown
18. spoke, spoken
19. threw, thrown
20. wondered, wondered

2. She graduated from college in 1994.
3. She's been reporting OR 's reported crime news since 1997.
4. Recently, she's been researching articles about crime in schools.
5. She's been working on her Master's Degree since 1997.
6. Her father worked for the Broadfield Police Department for twenty years.
7. Simon Pohlig moved to Broadfield in 1992.
8. He's owned Sharney's Restaurant since 1994.
9. He coached basketball for the Boys and Girls Club for two years.
10. He's written two cookbooks for children.
11. He's been planning a local television show for several months.
12. The groom's mother has been serving OR has served as president of TLC Meals, Inc., for two years.

2. applied
3. has been working OR has worked
4. found, was
5. has attended
6. began, received
7. went on
8. has been attending OR has attended
9. took
10. didn't get
11. decided
12. hasn't received
13. lived
14. has been living OR has lived
15. looked
16. left, mentioned
17. hasn't told OR didn't tell
18. didn't slant
19. told
20. suggested OR has suggested

My son and his girlfriend have ~~made~~ **been making** wedding

plans for the past few months. At first I was

delighted, but last week I ~~have heard~~ **heard** something

that changed my feelings. It seems that our future

daughter-in-law has ~~been deciding~~ **decided** to keep her

own last name after the wedding. Her reasons:

First, she doesn't want to "lose her identity." Her

parents ~~have named~~ **named** her 21 years ago, and she

~~was~~ **has been** Donna Esposito since then. She sees no

reason to change now. Second, she is a member

of the Rockland Symphony Orchestra and she

~~performed~~ **has performed** OR **has been performing** with them for eight years. As a result,

she ~~already became~~ **has already become** known professionally by her

maiden name.

John, when I've ~~gotten~~ **got** married, I didn't think

of keeping my maiden name. I ~~have felt~~ **felt** so proud

when I became "Mrs. Smith." We named our son

after my father, but our surname showed that we

three were a family.

I've ~~been reading~~ **read** two articles about this trend,

and I can now understand her decision to use her

maiden name professionally. But I still can't

understand why she wants to use it socially.

My husband and I ~~tried~~ **have been trying** OR **have tried** to hide our hurt feelings, but it's been getting harder. I want to tell her and my son what I think, but my husband says it's none of our business.

My son ~~didn't say~~ ^{hasn't said} anything, so we don't know how he feels. Have we ~~been making~~ ^{made} the right choice by keeping quiet?

~~HASN'T BEEN SAYING~~ ^{Hasn't said} ONE WORD YET

UNIT 4 PAST PERFECT AND PAST PERFECT PROGRESSIVE

1

3. entertained	12. led
4. cut	13. write
5. told	14. stolen
6. withdraw	15. planned
7. practiced	16. break
8. worried	17. swum
9. seek	18. bet
10. swept	19. sink
11. quit	20. forgiven

2

2. had enjoyed	9. had seen
3. had become	10. hadn't done
4. had started	11. had gotten
5. had . . . invented	12. hadn't been
6. hadn't appreciated	13. had grown
7. had written	14. hadn't seen
8. had been	15. had made

3

2. Had he driven, No, he hadn't.
3. Had he arrived, No, he hadn't.
4. Had he gone, Yes, he had.
5. Had he worked, Yes, he had.
6. Had he met, No, he hadn't.
7. Had he taped, Yes, he had.
8. Had he had OR eaten, No, he hadn't.
9. Had he gone, Yes, he had.

4

2. Before he appeared in New York City comedy clubs, he had gotten a part-time job as a car mechanic.
3. He wrote for TV after he had moved to Los Angeles.
4. By the time he appeared on "The Tonight Show," he had written for the TV show "Good Times."
5. He had appeared on "The Tonight Show" before he appeared on "Late Night with David Letterman."

6. When he got married, he had already appeared on "Late Night with David Letterman."
7. By the time he did his first prime-time TV show, he had performed at Carnegie Hall.
8. He had had a TV comedy special by the time he did his first prime-time TV show.
9. He had appeared on "The Tonight Show" many times when he became the permanent host of "The Tonight Show."

5

2. hadn't been doing	
3. had been telling	
4. had been raining	
5. had been eating	
6. hadn't been drinking	
7. had been crying	
8. had been laughing	
9. had been washing	
10. had been listening	
11. had been interviewing	
12. hadn't been paying	

6

1. Yes, I had.
2. Had . . . been crying, No, I hadn't.
3. Had . . . been expecting, No, I hadn't.
4. Had . . . been arguing, Yes, we had.
5. Had . . . been traveling, Yes, she had.
6. Had . . . been raining, No, it hadn't.

7

2. had immigrated
3. had been performing
4. had been working
5. (had been) going
6. had been entertaining
7. had . . . appeared
8. had been counting on
9. had created
10. had not represented
11. had learned

PART II FUTURE: REVIEW AND EXPANSION

UNIT 5 FUTURE AND FUTURE PROGRESSIVE

1

2. I'll come
3. Are you taking
4. I'll hand
5. It's going to fall
6. You're moving
7. Are you driving, We're flying

8. are you getting, We're going to take
9. I'll drive, we're going to have

2

2. will be living	10. won't be buying
3. will be parking	11. won't be paying
4. won't be preparing	12. won't be worrying
5. will be eating	13. will be providing
6. won't be driving	14. will be attending
7. will be walking	15. will be helping
8. will be moving	16. (will be) providing
9. will . . . be saving	17. will be seeing

3

2. will you be using the lawn mower tomorrow? No, I won't.
3. When will we be getting new washers?
4. will you be going to the post office tomorrow? Yes, I will.
5. What will you be making?
6. Who will be watching the kids tomorrow?
7. Will the entertainment committee be planning anything else in the near future? Yes, we will.
8. Will we be meeting every month? Yes, we will.
9. Will we be meeting then? No, we won't.

4

2. will be meeting with . . . faxes reports
3. attends . . . will be having a phone conference with John Smith
4. has OR eats . . . will be having OR eating lunch with Jack Allen
5. will be billing clients . . . drafts the A & W proposal
6. picks up . . . will be taking Saril to the dentist
7. will be shopping for . . . takes Dursan to the barber
8. pays . . . will be cutting the grass

5

I ~~go~~ **'m going** to Jack's with the kids in a few minutes. We'll be ~~play~~ **playing OR We're going to play** cards until 10:30 or so. While we'll ~~play~~ **'re playing OR we play** cards, Jack's daughter will be watching the kids. It ~~will~~ **'s going to** rain, so I closed all the windows. Don't forget to watch "ER"! It'll ~~start~~ **starts** at 10:00. I **'ll** call you after the card game because by the time we get home you're ~~sleeping~~ **'ll be sleeping.**

UNIT 6 FUTURE PERFECT AND FUTURE PERFECT PROGRESSIVE

1

2. will have completed
3. will have helped
4. will have been using
5. 'll have bought
6. 'll have wrapped
7. won't have planned
8. won't have decided
9. 'll . . . have been arguing
10. won't have wasted
11. 'll have completed
12. 'll have had
13. 'll have participated
14. (will have) redecorated
15. 'll have made
16. 'll have . . . done
17. 'll have straightened
18. 'll have packed
19. 'll have been explaining

2

1. Yes, I will (have).
2. will . . . have been singing
3. will . . . have sewn
4. will . . . have been waiting
5. will . . . have dried, No, it won't (have).
6. Will . . . have delivered, Yes, they will (have).
7. will . . . have been living OR have lived

3

2. A: How long will Aida have been walking by August 31?
   B: She'll have been walking (for) a month.
3. A: How many rooms will Arnie have painted by August 5?
   B: He'll have painted three rooms.
4. A: How long will Arnie have been painting downstairs by August 15?
   B: He'll have been painting downstairs (for) four days.
5. A: On August 16, will Arnie have left for his dentist appointment by four o'clock?
   B: Yes, he will (have).
6. A: Will Aida have unpacked all the fall clothing by August 23?
   B: No, she won't (have).
7. A: How long will Aida have been driving in the carpool by August 19?
   B: She'll have been driving in the carpool (for) two weeks.
8. A: How many quarts of blueberries will Corrie have picked by August 19?
   B: She'll have picked three quarts of blueberries.

9. A: How many pies will Aida have baked by
August 21?
B: She'll have baked six pies.
10. A: Will they have finished packing for the trip
by August 31?
B: Yes, they will (have).

PART ⫴ NEGATIVE QUESTIONS AND TAG QUESTIONS, ADDITIONS AND RESPONSES

UNIT 7 NEGATIVE *YES/NO* QUESTIONS AND TAG QUESTIONS

1

2. doesn't it? No, it doesn't.
3. is it? No, it isn't.
4. haven't you? Yes, I have.
5. does it? Yes, it does.
6. didn't you? Yes, I did.
7. isn't there? Yes, there is.
8. can we? Yes, you can.
9. will you? No, I won't.
10. don't you? Yes, I do.

2

2. Doesn't Greenwood have a public beach? No,
it doesn't.
3. Isn't there an airport in Greenwood? No, there
isn't.
4. Can't you see live theater in Greenwood? No,
you can't.
5. Don't people in Greenwood shop at the mall?
Yes, they do.
6. Isn't the average rent in Greenwood under
$700? Yes, it is.
7. Hasn't Greenwood been a town for more than
a hundred years? Yes, it has.
8. Aren't they going to build a baseball stadium
in Greenwood? Yes, they are.

3

1. c. 's
2. a. haven't seen
   b. Didn't . . . fill out
   c. shouldn't it
3. a. Isn't
   b. Didn't . . . use to be
   c. hadn't been
4. a. aren't they
   b. have you
   c. Can't . . . take

4

3. This is a good building, isn't it? OR Isn't this a
good building?
4. The owner takes good care of it, doesn't he?
OR Doesn't the owner take good care of it?
5. He recently redid the lobby, didn't he? OR
Didn't he recently redo the lobby?
6. He doesn't talk very much, does he?
7. The rent won't increase next year, will it?
8. There aren't many vacant apartments, are
there?
9. Some new people will be moving into
apartment 1B, won't they? OR Won't some new
people be moving into apartment 1B?
10. This is really a nice place to live, isn't it? OR
Isn't this really a nice place to live?

UNIT 8 ADDITIONS AND RESPONSES WITH *SO, TOO, NEITHER, NOT EITHER,* AND *BUT*

1

2. has	5. neither	8. do	11. don't
3. did	6. are	9. will	12. so
4. but	7. either	10. too	

2

2. did too	8. hasn't either
3. neither does	9. So does
4. so did	10. Neither can
5. couldn't either	11. So has
6. but . . . didn't	12. but . . . don't
7. so is	

3

2. but fish shouldn't
3. and so must dogs OR and dogs must too
4. and neither do fish OR and fish don't either
5. but birds and fish don't
6. but a fish doesn't
7. and so can a fish OR and a fish can too
8. and so will some fish OR and some fish will too
9. but other pets don't
10. and neither do fish OR and fish don't either
11. and so do cats OR and cats do too
12. and neither do birds OR and birds don't either

PART IV GERUNDS AND INFINITIVES

UNIT 9 GERUNDS AND INFINITIVES: REVIEW AND EXPANSION

❶

Verb + Gerund: enjoy, forget, stop, practice, recommend, quit, dislike, avoid, love, remember, hate, consider, prefer, give up, feel like

Verb + Infinitive: want, forget, stop, prepare, offer, need, love, remember, hate, decide, learn, promise, prefer, seem, manage

❷

2. watching
3. to recall
4. hearing
5. to calm
6. Sponsoring
7. to limit
8. to participate
9. creating
10. to preview
11. reducing
12. to believe
13. viewing
14. interacting
15. to behave
16. to produce
17. limiting
18. not permitting
19. to watch
20. to understand
21. making
22. to develop
23. (to) get rid of
24. not to make
25. not to continue
26. to avoid OR avoiding
27. not to pay
28. to investigate
29. to offer
30. turning on

❸

2. unwilling to change
3. used to putting
4. fed up with seeing
5. likely to hit
6. force . . . to rate
7. hesitate to tell
8. decided to run
9. stopped showing
10. dislike turning off
11. insist on changing
12. forbid turning on
13. permit tuning in
14. dream of owning
15. advise . . . to do
16. keep communicating
17. hesitate to ask
18. agreeing to speak

❹

2. A V-chip interferes with their OR them watching violent shows.
3. Beakman encourages them to send in OR their sending in questions.
4. The father objected to Jennifer's OR Jennifer watching cop shows.
5. The teacher recommended their watching "Nick News."
6. Bob didn't remember their OR them seeing that game.
7. Sharif's parents persuaded him not to watch "Z-Men."

8. The mother insisted on Sara's OR Sara turning off the TV.
9. Aziza wanted OR wants Ben to change the channel.
10. Paul can't understand Nick's OR Nick watching the show.

❺

I'm tired of ~~hear~~ **hearing** that violence on TV causes violence at home, in school, and on the streets. Almost all young people watch TV, but not all of them are involved in committing crimes! In fact, very few people choose ~~acting~~ **to act** in violent ways. ~~To watch~~ **Watching** TV, therefore, is not the cause.

Groups like the American Medical Society should stop ~~to try~~ **trying** to tell people what to watch. If we want ~~living~~ **to live** in a free society, it is necessary ~~having~~ **to have** freedom of choice. Children need ~~learn~~ **to learn** values from their parents. It should be the parents' responsibility ~~deciding~~ **to decide** what their child can or cannot watch. The government and other interest groups should avoid ~~to interfere~~ **interfering** in these personal decisions. Limiting our freedom of choice is not the answer. If parents teach their children ~~respecting~~ **to respect** life, children can enjoy ~~to watch~~ **watching** TV without any negative effects.

UNIT 10 MAKE, HAVE, LET, HELP, AND GET

❶

2. made
3. let
4. made
5. let
6. got
7. helped
8. had
9. made
10. have
11. made
12. let
13. made

❷

2. didn't let them take
3. had them answer
4. made them hand in
5. didn't let them submit
6. had them write
7. let them come
8. had them submit
9. made them sign
10. had them keep
11. didn't make them go
12. help them do OR to do

❸

2. made Mark OR him work it out himself.
3. made Sara OR her try again.
4. had Robert OR him do his homework OR it over.
5. didn't let the students OR them use a calculator.
6. got the students OR them to help clean up the classroom.

❹

      Mrs. Olinski made us ~~to stay~~ **stay** late again after class today. She wants to help us ~~passing~~ **pass OR to pass** our next test by giving us extra time to review in class. She won't ~~make~~ **let** us use calculators during the test. She says, "Calculators make students ~~to forget~~ **forget** how to add two plus two!" She's always trying to get us ~~use~~ **to use** our brains instead. She has us solve lots of homework problems, and she gets us ~~asking~~ **to ask** lots of questions in class. She's strict, but I think she's a good teacher. She's definitely dedicated. She even ~~lets~~ **lets** us call her at home. She's certainly gotten me to learn more than I ever did before. Now, if she could only get me to enjoy math, that would really be an accomplishment!

PART V PHRASAL VERBS

UNIT 11 PHRASAL VERBS: REVIEW

❶

2. up	6. down	10. out	14. down
3. over	7. over	11. up	
4. ahead	8. out	12. down	
5. out	9. back	13. up	

❷

2. cut down	7. gets together
3. put together	8. give out
4. burns up	9. go out
5. sets up	10. go back
6. puts on	11. throws away

❸

1. pick them out
2. empty them out, throw it away
3. set them off, keeps them away
4. hanging them up, set it up
5. write them down, gave them up

❹

Wake ~~out~~ **up** earlier. (No later than 7:30!)

Work out in the gym at least three times a week.

Lose five pounds. (Give ~~over~~ **up** eating so many desserts.)

Be more conscious of the environment—
  —Don't throw ~~down~~ **away OR out** newspapers. Recycle them.
  —Save energy. Turn ~~on~~ **off OR out** the lights when I leave
    the apartment.

Straighten up my room.
  —Hang ~~out~~ **up** my clothes when I take ~~off them~~ **them off**.
  —Put my books back where they belong.
  —Give some of my old books and clothing that
    I no longer wear ~~away~~ **away**.

Don't put off doing my homework assignments.
Hand ~~in them~~ **them in** on time!

Read more.

Use the dictionary more. (Look ~~over~~ **up** words I
don't know.)

When someone calls and leaves a message, call
them back right away. Don't put ~~off it~~ **it off**!

Get to know my neighbors. Ask them for coffee
~~over~~ **over**.

UNIT 12 PHRASAL VERBS: SEPARABLE AND INSEPARABLE

❶

2. over	8. into
3. out	9. up
4. off	10. over
5. in (on) OR by	11. out OR away
6. out	12. back
7. on	13. out

2

1. b. figure out
   c. carried out
   d. did . . . over
   e. handed out
   f. caught on
   g. calling . . . up
   h. give up
   i. set up

2. a. grown up
   b. ended up
   c. put together
   d. turned on
   e. pushed up
   f. found out
   g. come up with
   h. brought out
   i. caught on

3

2. get along (well) with him
3. run into her
4. straighten it up
5. get through with it
6. pick them OR some out
7. run out of it
8. bring it out
9. picked it up
10. turn it down
11. cover them up
12. used them up
13. put them away
14. turn it on
15. figure it out

4

PART VI ADJECTIVE CLAUSES

UNIT 13 ADJECTIVE CLAUSES WITH SUBJECT RELATIVE PRONOUNS

1

2. whose
3. who
4. who
5. that
6. who
7. whose
8. which
9. who
10. that
11. whose
12. who
13. that
14. who

2

1. c. that OR which
   d. occur
   e. who OR that
   f. stay
   g. who OR that
   h. make
2. a. that OR which
   b. don't change
   c. that OR which
   d. remain
   e. whose
   f. end
   g. who OR that
3. a. that OR which
   b. helps
4. a. that OR which
   b. makes
   c. that OR which
   d. holds

5. a. that OR which
   b. surrounds
   c. who OR that
   d. know
6. a. that OR which
   b. has
7. a. who OR that
   b. has
   c. whose
   d. are
   e. who OR that
   f. consider
   g. who OR that
   h. seize

3

2. She was visiting her aunt, whose apartment was right across from mine. OR She was visiting her aunt whose apartment was right across from mine.
3. I loved Rebecca's smile, which was full of warmth and good humor.
4. We shared a lot of interests that OR which brought us close together.
5. We both enjoyed ballroom dancing, which was very popular then.
6. We also enjoyed playing cards with some of our friends who lived in the neighborhood.
7. Our friend Mike, who was a professional skier, taught us how to ski.
8. We got married in a ski lodge that OR which was in Vermont.
9. Our marriage, which means a lot to us both, has grown through the years.
10. We have two children, who are both in school.
11. We both have jobs that OR which are important to us.
12. I really love Rebecca, who is not only my wife but also my best friend.

UNIT **ADJECTIVE CLAUSES WITH OBJECT RELATIVE PRONOUNS OR *WHEN* AND *WHERE***

1

1. **b.** who
2. **a.** who
   b. who
   c. whom
3. **a.** who
   b. who
   c. whose
4. **a.** who
   b. where
   c. whom
5. **a.** which
   b. whose
   c. whom
   d. whose
   e. that

6. **a.** that
   b. where
   c. who
7. **a.** whose
   b. whose
   c. who
   d. which
   e. who
   f. whom

2

2. where
3. thanks
4. whose
5. has found OR found
6. which OR that
7. writes
8. which OR that
9. reads
10. which OR that
11. face
12. when OR that
13. runs out OR has run out
14. when
15. supported
16. which
17. praised
18. which
19. inserted
20. whom
21. feels
22. whom
23. dedicates OR has dedicated
24. where
25. has
26. which OR that
27. 're supposed to

3

2. *The Clan of the Cave Bear,* which Auel started researching in 1977, tells the story of a clan of prehistoric people.
3. The clan lived during the Ice Age, when glaciers covered large parts of the earth.
4. The story takes place during a period in the Ice Age when the climate was slightly warmer.

5. The people lived near the shores of the Black Sea, where there are a lot of large caves.
6. Bears, which the clan worshiped, lived in some of the caves.
7. The clan made their home in a large cave in which OR where bears had lived. OR which OR that bears had lived in.
8. One aspect of their lives which OR that Auel describes well is their technical skill.
9. She learned some of the arts that OR which prehistoric people had practiced.
10. In her preface, she thanks a man with whom she studied the art of making stone tools. OR she thanks a man who OR whom OR that she studied the art of making stone tools with.
11. She also thanks an Artic survival expert who OR whom OR that she met while she was doing research.
12. He taught her to make a snow cave on Mt. Hood, where she spent one January night.
13. She went through a difficult time when she couldn't write.
14. A fiction writer whose lecture she attended inspired her to finish her book.
15. *The Clan of the Cave Bear,* which Auel published in 1980, was a best-seller for a long time.

4

Sentence 8: One aspect of their lives Auel describes well is their technical skill.
Sentence 9: She learned some of the arts prehistoric people had practiced.
Sentence 10: In her preface, she thanks a man she studied the art of making stone tools with.
Sentence 11: She also thanks an Arctic survival expert she met while she was doing research.

5

For my book report, I read *The Clan of the Cave Bear* by Jean M. Auel. This novel, ~~that~~ which is about the life of prehistoric people, took years to research. The main character is Ayla. She is found by a wandering clan after an earthquake kills her family. The same earthquake had destroyed the cave in which this clan had lived, and they are searching for another home. The clan leader wants to leave Ayla to die. She is an Other—a human whose ~~which~~ language and culture his clan doesn't understand. However, the leader's sister Iza, who OR whom ~~whose~~ Ayla soon calls Mother, adopts her.

The story takes place at a time ~~where~~ *when* human beings are still evolving. Ayla is a new kind of human. Her brain, ~~that~~ *which* she can use to predict and make plans, is different from Iza's and other clan members'. Their brains are adapted to memory, not new learning, ~~whom~~ *which* they fear and distrust. At first, Ayla brings luck to the clan. She accidentally wanders into a place where they find a large cave, perfect for their new home. She is educated by Iza, ~~who's~~ *whose* great knowledge everyone respects. The skills that Iza passes on to Ayla include healing and magic, as well as finding food, cooking, and sewing. However, Ayla's powers make it impossible for her to stay with the clan. She learns to hunt, a skill ~~where~~ *which OR that OR (pronoun deleted)* women are forbidden to practice. Her uncle, ~~that~~ *who OR whom* she loves very much, allows her to stay with the clan, but after he dies, she loses his protection. Another earthquake, for which she is blamed, destroys the clan's home, and she is forced to leave.

TEST: UNITS 1–4

PART ONE

DIRECTIONS: Circle the letter of the correct answer to complete each sentence.

EXAMPLE:

Mark _____ a headache last night.   (A) B C D
   (A) had   (C) has had
   (B) has   (D) was having

1. Her name is Victoria, but her friends   A B C D
   _____ her Vicki.
   (A) are calling   (C) had called
   (B) call   (D) were calling

2. Water _____ at 0 degrees C.   A B C D
   (A) freezes   (C) has been freezing
   (B) froze   (D) is freezing

3. In her latest book, the author _____   A B C D
   her childhood.
   (A) describes   (C) has been describing
   (B) is describing   (D) was describing

4. John _____. It really annoys me.   A B C D
   (A) always complain   (C) is always complaining
   (B) had always complained   (D) was always complaining

5. I _____ Jackie, but I didn't.   A B C D
   (A) told   (C) was going to tell
   (B) 've told   (D) was telling

6. By 11:00 this morning, I _____   A B C D
   three cups of coffee.
   (A) drink   (C) had drunk
   (B) had been drinking   (D) have drunk

7. I was listening to the radio when I _____   A B C D
   the news.
   (A) hear   (C) 've heard
   (B) heard   (D) was hearing

8. They _____ in Paris when they met for the first time.   **A B C D**
   - (A) lived
   - (B) 've lived
   - (C) 've been living
   - (D) were living

9. Sara always _____ glasses. She can't see without them.   **A B C D**
   - (A) had worn
   - (B) has been wearing
   - (C) is wearing
   - (D) wears

10. Can you please turn down the radio? The baby _____.   **A B C D**
    - (A) has slept
    - (B) is sleeping
    - (C) sleeps
    - (D) slept

11. The Morrisons _____ to Texas last September.   **A B C D**
    - (A) had moved
    - (B) have been moving
    - (C) have moved
    - (D) moved

12. While Jedd was living in Toronto, Helen _____ in California.   **A B C D**
    - (A) has lived
    - (B) had lived
    - (C) lives
    - (D) was living

Part Two

DIRECTIONS: Each sentence has four underlined words or phrases. The four underlined parts of the sentence are marked A, B, C, and D. Circle the letter of the <u>one</u> underlined word or phrase that is NOT CORRECT.

Example:

Rosa <u>rarely</u> <u>is using</u> public transportation, but <u>this morning</u> she   **A Ⓑ C D**
      A   B   C

<u>is taking</u> the bus.
   D

13. The doctor <u>called</u> <u>this morning</u> <u>while</u> you <u>slept</u>.   **A B C D**
              A   B   C   D

14. <u>When</u> she <u>was</u> little, they <u>were naming</u> her "Strawberry" because   **A B C D**
       A   B   C

    she <u>had</u> beautiful red hair.
         D

15. They <u>were going to</u> <u>drive</u> to the beach, but they <u>have changed</u> their   **A B C D**
          A   B   C

    plans when it <u>started</u> to rain.
           D

16. <u>By the time</u> I <u>had gotten</u> home, the show <u>had</u> <u>already ended</u>.   **A B C D**
        A   B   C   D

17. Pete and Andy <u>were</u> <u>driving</u> to work <u>when</u> they <u>were seeing</u> the   **A   B   C   D**
              A   B   C   D

      accident.

18. Erika <u>has</u> <u>been looking</u> for a job <u>since</u> she <u>has graduated</u> from college.   **A   B   C   D**
        A   B   C   D

19. Janice <u>didn't own</u> a car then because she <u>hasn't</u> <u>learned</u> to drive <u>yet</u>.   **A   B   C   D**
           A   B   C   D

20. I <u>had</u> <u>been living</u> in this apartment for ten years, but <u>I'm</u> <u>looking</u> for   **A   B   C   D**
      A   B   C   D

      a new one now.

TEST: UNITS 5–6

DIRECTIONS: Circle the letter of the correct answer to complete each sentence.

EXAMPLE:

Mark _____ a headache last night.   (A) B C D
   (A) had   (C) has had
   (B) has   (D) was having

1. Bill will be _____ to Taipei tomorrow.   A B C D
   (A) flies   (C) fly
   (B) flying   (D) have been flying

2. We _____ a new TV soon.   A B C D
   (A) had owned   (C) 're owning
   (B) 'll own   (D) 've owned

3. Look at those dark clouds! It _____.   A B C D
   (A) rains   (C) 's raining
   (B) 's going to rain   (D) will rain

4. They'll be making photocopies while he   A B C D
   _____ typing the report.
   (A) finishes   (C) 'll finish
   (B) 'll be finishing   (D) 's been finishing

5. I _____ be working tomorrow. I'll be   A B C D
   out of town.
   (A) don't   (C) 'm not
   (B) haven't   (D) won't

6. Kareem will _____ almost $1,000 by   A B C D
   next year.
   (A) had saved   (C) have saved
   (B) have been saving (D) saves

7. We're late. When we _____ there, they'll   A B C D
   already have eaten dinner.
   (A) get   (C) 'll get
   (B) got   (D) 'll have gotten

8. By the end of this week, Henry _____ regularly for   **A B C D**
six months.
   (A) exercised   (C) will exercise
   (B) exercises   (D) will have been exercising

9. When I finish this mystery story by Nguyen Treng, I'll   **A B C D**
_____ all of her mysteries.
   (A) be reading   (C) have read
   (B) have been reading   (D) read

10. Next year, the Carters will have been living in that house   **A B C D**
_____ forty years.
   (A) already   (C) since
   (B) for   (D) yet

PART TWO

DIRECTIONS: Each sentence has four underlined words or phrases. The four underlined parts of the sentence are marked A, B, C, and D. Circle the letter of the <u>one</u> underlined word or phrase that is NOT CORRECT.

EXAMPLE:

Rosa <u>rarely</u> <u>is using</u> public transportation, but <u>this morning</u> she   **A Ⓑ C D**
      A   B   C
<u>is taking</u> the bus.
   D

11. <u>Will</u> you <u>been</u> <u>going</u> to the drugstore <u>tonight</u>?   **A B C D**
     A   B   C   D

12. <u>While</u> Bill <u>will wash</u> the dishes, <u>I'll</u> be <u>straightening</u> the living room.   **A B C D**
     A   B   C   D

13. <u>After</u> I <u>finished</u> this lap, <u>I'll have</u> <u>walked</u> three miles.   **A B C D**
     A   B   C   D

14. Professor Sanek <u>is</u> <u>arriving</u> at 8:00, and he <u>calls</u> you <u>then</u>.   **A B C D**
                  A   B   C   D

15. The Tokagarus <u>will save</u> <u>for</u> ten years <u>by the time</u> their first   **A B C D**
                   A   B   C
child <u>enters</u> college.
       D

16. Seana will <u>has</u> <u>been</u> watching television <u>for</u> an hour by the time   **A B C D**
          A   B   C
dinner <u>is</u> ready.
      D

17. In the twenty-first century, most <u>people</u> in this country <u>will</u> <u>be</u> <u>work</u>   **A B C D**
                                    A   B C D
in service jobs.

18. At the end of this year, Tania <u>will</u> <u>have</u> been <u>paying</u> her credit card   **A B C D**
                                             A   B   C

   bill <u>since</u> three years.
        D

19. She<u>'ll</u> <u>have</u> <u>been paying</u> a total of $3,000 by the time she <u>pays off</u>   **A B C D**
      A B   C   D

   her loan.

20. John loves that old suitcase. By the time he <u>gets</u> home from vacation   **A B C D**
                                                  A

   <u>next month</u>, he'll <u>have</u> <u>carries</u> it at least 50,000 miles.
      B   C   D

TEST: UNITS 7–8

PART ONE

DIRECTIONS: Circle the letter of the correct answer to complete each sentence.

EXAMPLE:

Mark _____ a headache last night.   Ⓐ B C D
- (A) had
- (B) has
- (C) has had
- (D) was having

1. _____ you from Panama?   A B C D
   - (A) Aren't
   - (B) Come
   - (C) Did
   - (D) Didn't

2. Ben's not at work today, _____?   A B C D
   - (A) does he
   - (B) doesn't he
   - (C) is he
   - (D) isn't he

3. Your cousin lived in New York, _____?   A B C D
   - (A) didn't she
   - (B) hadn't she
   - (C) isn't she
   - (D) wasn't she

4. Miguel _____ here very long, has he?   A B C D
   - (A) has been
   - (B) hasn't been
   - (C) was
   - (D) wasn't

5. **A:** Doesn't Sam own a house in Florida?   A B C D
   B: _____ He bought one there last year.
   - (A) No, he doesn't.
   - (B) No, he didn't.
   - (C) Yes, he does.
   - (D) Yes, he did.

6. **A:** Can't Rick speak Spanish?   A B C D
   B: _____ He never learned.
   - (A) No, he can't.
   - (B) No, he doesn't.
   - (C) Yes, he can.
   - (D) Yes, he does.

7. That's your notebook, isn't _____?   A B C D
   - (A) there
   - (B) it
   - (C) yours
   - (D) that

8. **A:** You're not Alex, are you?   A   B   C   D
   B: _____ I'm Alex Winslow.
   (A) No, I'm not.   (C) Yes, I am.
   (B) No, you're not.   (D) Yes, you are.

9. **A:** Today's July 5th, isn't it?   A   B   C   D
   B: _____ It's the 6th.
   (A) Neither is it.   (C) So is it.
   (B) No, it isn't.   (D) Yes, it is.

10. They've read the paper, _____ I have too.   A   B   C   D
    (A) and   (C) either
    (B) but   (D) neither

11. **A:** Jennifer ate at home last night.   A   B   C   D
    B: _____ I saw him having dinner in the school cafeteria.
    (A) But Mike did.   (C) Neither did Mike.
    (B) But Mike didn't.   (D) So did Mike.

12. **A:** Andrea speaks fluent French.   A   B   C   D
    B: _____
    (A) Neither does Paul.   (C) So is Paul.
    (B) So does Paul.   (D) So Paul does.

13. **A:** The Mets played well last night.   A   B   C   D
    B: So _____ the Phillies. It was an exciting game.
    (A) did   (C) played
    (B) didn't   (D) were

14. The hotel _____ expensive, and so were the restaurants.   A   B   C   D
    (A) was   (C) were
    (B) wasn't   (D) weren't

PART TWO

DIRECTIONS: Each sentence has four underlined words or phrases. The four underlined parts of the sentence are marked A, B, C, and D. Circle the letter of the <u>one</u> underlined word or phrase that is NOT CORRECT.

EXAMPLE:

Rosa <u>rarely</u> <u>is using</u> public transportation, but <u>this morning</u> she   A (B) C   D
     A   B   C
<u>is taking</u> the bus.
   D

15. <u>This</u> <u>isn't</u> the way to Route 101, <u>is</u> <u>this</u>?   A   B   C   D
    A   B   C D

16. Mary <u>works</u> on Saturdays, <u>doesn't</u> <u>Mary</u>?   A   B   C   D
          A   B C   D

17. Jeff <u>bought</u> a new car, <u>and</u> <u>so</u> <u>does</u> Ann.
      A   B C D
            A B C D

18. Rachel <u>didn't</u> <u>go</u> to class today, <u>and</u> her sister <u>did</u>.
            A   B   C   D
            A B C D

19. I <u>didn't enjoy</u> the movie, <u>and</u> Frank <u>did</u> <u>either</u>.
       A   B   C D
            A B C D

20. Vilma <u>is coming</u> to the party, <u>and</u> <u>so</u> <u>Craig is</u>.
       A   B C   D
            A B C D

TEST: UNITS 9–10

DIRECTIONS: Circle the letter of the correct answer to complete each sentence.

EXAMPLE:

Mark _____ a headache last night.   (A) B C D
    (A) had   (C) has had
    (B) has   (D) was having

1. _____ the streets safe again is the   A B C D
   mayor's highest priority.
       (A) Is making   (C) Makes
       (B) Make   (D) Making

2. Geraldo is looking forward to _____   A B C D
   a father.
       (A) became   (C) becomes
       (B) becoming   (D) become

3. It was very difficult _____ a good job.   A B C D
       (A) find   (C) has found
       (B) found   (D) to find

4. Elliot bought an exercise video _____   A B C D
   him get into shape.
       (A) helped   (C) is helping
       (B) helps   (D) to help

5. It's time _____ where we want to go   A B C D
   this summer.
       (A) to decide   (C) deciding
       (B) decides   (D) decide

6. I'm sorry, but I forgot _____ that book   A B C D
   you asked for.
       (A) bring   (C) to bring
       (B) bringing   (D) brought

7. I can't imagine _____ that.   A B C D
       (A) do   (C) you to do
       (B) to do   (D) your doing

8. Pat invited _____ the weekend with them.   **A   B   C   D**
   (A) I spend   (C) me to spend
   (B) me spend   (D) my spending

9. The judge made the witness _____ the question.   **A   B   C   D**
   (A) answer   (C) answering
   (B) answered   (D) to answer

10. It's a good idea _____ a reservation.   **A   B   C   D**
    (A) make   (C) made
    (B) makes   (D) to make

11. The defendant denied _____ a weapon.   **A   B   C   D**
    (A) owned   (C) owns
    (B) owning   (D) to own

12. Gary didn't write down the test date, so he didn't   **A   B   C   D**
    remember _____.
    (A) studied   (C) studying
    (B) studies   (D) to study

PART TWO

DIRECTIONS: Each sentence has four underlined words or phrases. The four underlined parts of the sentence are marked A, B, C, and D. Circle the letter of the <u>one</u> underlined word or phrase that is NOT CORRECT.

EXAMPLE:

Rosa <u>rarely</u> <u>is using</u> public transportation, but <u>this morning</u> she   **A   Ⓑ
  C   D**
      A   B   C
<u>is taking</u> the bus.
     D

13. I <u>got</u> all my friends <u>help</u> <u>me</u> <u>move</u> last June.   **A   B   C   D**
      A   B   C   D

14. Phil decided <u>changing</u> jobs because his boss always <u>made</u> <u>him</u>   **A   B   C   D**
                      A   B   C
    <u>work</u> overtime.
     D

15. The students of Maitlin High <u>appreciated</u> their <u>principal's</u> <u>try</u>   **A   B   C   D**
                                 A   B   C
    <u>to improve</u> conditions in their school.
     D

16. Sally is really tired <u>for</u> <u>being</u> responsible for <u>everyone's</u> <u>doing</u> the   **A   B   C   D**
                         A   B   C   D
    work on time.

17. Robert <u>succeeded in</u> <u>to find</u> a job after high school, so his parents   **A   B   C   D**
             A   B
    <u>didn't make</u> him <u>apply</u> to college.
       C   D

Test: Units 9–10 **T12**

18. If you insist <u>on</u> <u>looking</u> over the report, please <u>don't forget</u> <u>returning</u>   **A B C D**
                A   B   C   D
it by Monday.

19. <u>Going</u> on a diet doesn't <u>seem</u> <u>to be</u> the best way <u>losing</u> weight.   **A B C D**
   A   B   C   D

20. If you're <u>planning</u> <u>to be</u> near the post office today, <u>could</u> you stop   **A B C D**
           A   B   C
<u>buying</u> some stamps?
  D

TEST: UNITS 11–12

PART ONE

DIRECTIONS: Circle the letter of the correct answer to complete each sentence.

EXAMPLE:

Mark _____ a headache last night.   (Ⓐ) B C D
   (A) had   (C) has had
   (B) has   (D) was having

1. Jan was depressed when the company she wanted   A B C D
   to work for turned _____ her application
   for the job.
   (A) down   (C) on
   (B) off   (D) out

2. Your mother called. She wants you to call   A B C D
   her _____ tonight.
   (A) back   (C) off
   (B) in   (D) over

3. That's very original. How did you dream   A B C D
   _____ that idea?
   (A) about   (C) of
   (B) down   (D) up

4. **A:** It's cold outside. You need your jacket.   A B C D
   B: OK. I'll put _____.
   (A) it on   (C) on it
   (B) it over   (D) over it

5. Some damage was brought _____ by   A B C D
   high winds.
   (A) about   (C) down
   (B) across   (D) through

6. Come in. Please sit _____.   A B C D
   (A) down   (C) it down
   (B) down it   (D) up

7. Every spring, Marta _____ away some clothes to a local charity.　　　　　　　　　　　　　　**A B C D**
   (A) gives   (C) puts
   (B) keeps   (D) throws

8. I can hardly hear the TV. Could you turn it _____?　　**A B C D**
   (A) in   (C) on
   (B) off   (D) up

9. She ran _____ on the way to the supermarket.　　**A B C D**
   (A) him into   (C) into Jason
   (B) into   (D) Jason into

10. It's too cold to take your mittens off. _____　　**A B C D**
    (A) Don't keep them on.   (C) Keep them.
    (B) Keep on.   (D) Keep them on.

11. Erika wants to quit, but she says she'll _____.　　**A B C D**
    (A) give up   (C) see through the project
    (B) see the project through   (D) see through it

PART TWO

DIRECTIONS: Each sentence has four underlined words or phrases. The four underlined parts of the sentence are marked A, B, C, and D. Circle the letter of the <u>one</u> underlined word or phrase that is NOT CORRECT.

EXAMPLE:

Rosa <u>rarely</u> <u>is using</u> public transportation, but <u>this morning</u> she　　(A) **B C D**
　　　　A　　　B　　　　　　　　　　　　　　　　C
<u>is taking</u> the bus.
　　D

12. Could we talk <u>over it</u> before you <u>turn</u> the whole <u>idea</u> <u>down</u>?　　**A B C D**
　　　　　　　　　A　　　　　　　B　　　　　　C　　D

13. I know I <u>let</u> <u>Andy</u> <u>down</u> when I forgot to pick his suit <u>out</u> from the　　**A B C D**
　　　　　　A　　B　　C　　　　　　　　　　　　　　　　D
    dry cleaner's.

14. I <u>ran into</u> <u>him</u> when I was <u>getting</u> <u>the bus off</u>.　　**A B C D**
　　　A　　　　B　　　　　　　　C　　　D

15. As soon as I <u>hand</u> <u>in</u> <u>my report</u>, I'm going to take all these books　　**A B C D**
　　　　　　　　A　　B　　C
    <u>on</u> to the library.
　　D

16. When you <u>come across</u> <u>a new word</u>, it's a good idea to <u>look it</u>　　**A B C D**
　　　　　　　A　　　　　　B　　　　　　　　　　　　　C
    <u>in a dictionary up</u>.
　　　　D

17. <u>We'd better</u> <u>get the bus on</u> now, or <u>we</u>'re going to <u>miss it</u>.   **A B C D**
    A   B   C   D

18. Instead of <u>calling</u> <u>off</u> the meeting, maybe we can just <u>put it</u> <u>over</u>   **A B C D**
            A   B   C   D
until next week.

19. If you don't use <u>out</u> the milk by Monday, please <u>throw</u> <u>it</u> <u>away</u>.   **A B C D**
                          A   B C D

20. Greg <u>had to</u> <u>cheer up her</u> after the company <u>turned down</u>   **A B C D**
           A   B   C
<u>her application</u>.
     D